Merry Christmas,

Fay

BRIAN'S BENEDICTION
A Book of Daily Devotions

by Brian Giese

DORRANCE
PUBLISHING CO
EST. 1920
PITTSBURGH, PENNSYLVANIA 15238

Dorrance Publishing Co
585 Alpha Drive
Pittsburgh, PA 15238
Visit our website at *www.dorrancebookstore.com*

ISBN: 978-1-6453-0101-1
eISBN: 978-1-6453-0067-0

TABLE OF CONTENTS

INTRODUCTION

The title of this book is taken from a column written by me for sixteen years in our church paper. I chose to call it *Brian's Benediction* for two reasons. First, it was the final item on the back page of the paper, just as a prayer of benediction closes a worship service. Second, it was intended to be a blessing. The word "benediction" is the Latin form for the word "blessing". It means "to say (dicere) good things (bene)".

Hopefully, those who read the following pages will be spiritually blessed. I have adapted the church paper articles to a devotional format which includes a scripture reading and prayer thoughts.

Over the years, this writer has often used devotional books and periodicals to supplement his daily reading of Scripture. My spiritual development has been enhanced by these readings. Many years ago, I began praying that God would enable me to write such a book. To Him be the glory for honoring that prayer!

—Brian Giese

DEDICATION

This book is dedicated to my beloved wife, Sylvia, who took my rough drafts and made them smooth. This book never would have happened without her work at the keyboard and words of encouragement.

Acknowledgments

In addition to my wife, Sylvia (mentioned in the Dedication), I owe a debt of gratitude to Merry Ann Malcolm (friend) and Katie Yankey (daughter) who proofread everything and made needed corrections and helpful suggestions.

Thanks are also due to Austin and Annie Boswell for their fine art work on the book's front cover.

Special thanks also is due to two men who encouraged me in my writing as a young man. Praise God for Sam Stone and Orin Root, both highly gifted editors and mentors.

WHERE WILL YOU FIND JOY?

SCRIPTURE READING - Nehemiah 8:10; Romans 14:17

Joy is often found in unlikely places. As one who has spent many hours visiting in hospitals and nursing homes, I can tell you that some seriously hurting people still radiate joy. What a testimony it is for a very ill or seriously disabled person to still be caring for and encouraging others.

You see, there is joy and then there is JOY. There is a joy of the world that is temporary and shallow and does not impact lives for good and for God. True joy, however, is of the Holy Spirit. You cannot have the fruit of the Spirit unless you have the Holy Spirit Himself within you. Joy is one facet of the Holy Spirit's fruit. (Galatians 5:22).

Joy is not to be confused with happiness. Happiness has to do with happenings. When things are going well with my family, the bills are paid, I like my job, and am physically healthy, I feel happy. Biblical joy, however, is possible when everything is going wrong. Such joy is much deeper than happiness. It is an inner sense of peace, serenity, and serendipity. You know that you are the Lord's and He is yours. You are confident that all things are working out for the good. As one of my seminary professors used to say, "The worst thing that could happen to you may be the best thing that could happen to you, if you don't let the worst get the best of you."

PRAYER THOUGHTS - Gracious Heavenly Father, thank You for

divine joy which keeps us strong even when we are weak. May we never settle for the joy of this world which is merely a cheap imitation of what You offer us.

THE PRIORITY OF PRAYER

SCRIPTURE READING - James 4:1-3

Prayer is not a high priority for many Christians. A national poll showed that the average Christian only prays three minutes a day. That is not good news. We cannot have victory in our lives and churches with that level of praying.

Prayer focuses on God's desires rather than what we want. Prayer needs to be our first response rather than our last resort. We should make our plans with prayer rather than praying out of desperation when our plans fail.

Prayer is how God gets things done. God is all-powerful, but He has decided that He is not going to do much unless we ask Him, (James 4:2). In this way, He teaches us to develop a Kingdom mentality. God told Ezekiel He wanted to find someone to stand in the gap so He would not have to destroy Israel, (Ezekiel 22:30). God could not find anyone.

What does God refuse to do because we are not praying for it? What is happening that God does not want to happen because nobody is praying about it? Prayer is the work of Christians. How well will we do the work of God this week? How much of God's purpose and plan for our community is being fulfilled or not being fulfilled because of our level of praying?

PRAYER THOUGHTS - Heavenly Father, we declare our dependence upon You for every good and perfect gift. Forgive us for the times You have been unable to bless us because we have failed to ask.

ARE YOU AN EVANGELIST?

SCRIPTURE READING - Daniel 12:1-3

Many different methods are used to share the Gospel and not all of them are equally effective. Some people feel evangelism works best when you push people to commit their lives to Christ. They may even use manipulative methods to reach this goal. No wonder many of us feel a strange sensation in our stomachs when we hear the word "evangelism". But evangelism is not selling. We are called to be servants, not salesmen. You do not find Jesus and the apostles selling.

Evangelism is also not a method or an event, it is something you are. This is not passive evangelism, hoping to reach people for Christ by merely setting a good example. We are to make disciples. There is a time to talk. The Great Commission in Matthew 28:19-20 commands us to make disciples and to teach them to obey all that Christ taught.

It is not enough to help people to be born again. Birth is not the end, it is the means to new life. We do not want our children to die the day they are born. We want them to grow, thrive, and fulfill their potential. We should help "baby" Christians to do the same.

PRAYER THOUGHTS - Lord, you gave us an example by investing yourself in the lives of your disciples for three years. Help us to go and do likewise.

WHY BE BAPTIZED?

SCRIPTURE READING - Matthew 3:13-17

What is the purpose of baptism? Some teach that baptism alone saves you so they baptize infants. Others claim that baptism has nothing to do with salvation, but is only for local church membership and/or as a public testimony of one's faith. But the Bible teaches that baptism is a part of saving faith, (Mark 16:16; Acts 8:12-13; 18:8, Galatians 3:26-27).

Not only does the Bible connect baptism with faith, it also connects it with repentance, (Mark 1:4; Acts 2:38). Nationally-known pastor Jack Hayford said, "When somebody asks me, 'Do I have to be baptized?' I ask them, 'Why do you want to be rebellious?' I then explain to them that the Bible associates baptism with repentance and I ask, 'Have you really repented if you are not willing to obey the Lord's command to be baptized?'"

If the Bible is so clear, why are so many confused? One reason is that there is a lot of single-verse theology going on. For example, someone quotes John 3:16 and says, "That is the whole plan of salvation. All you need to do is believe."

However, if we are to properly interpret Scripture, we need to process everything it says on a given subject. When you study the New Testament, you learn that salvation is promised when you believe in Christ, confess your faith, repent of your sins, and are buried with Christ in the watery grave of baptism. Let's do all that God requires so that we may rejoice in our salvation.

PRAYER THOUGHTS - Heavenly Father, as Jesus was baptized to "fulfill all righteousness," so may each of us be.

YOUR SECOND-
MOST IMPORTANT DECISION

SCRIPTURE READING - 2 Corinthians 6:14-18

One of the greatest assets in this writer's life has been a good and faithful helpmate. I am thankful that my parents taught me that next to choosing Christ as my Savior, the most important decision I would ever make would be choosing a life partner.

For that reason, I was quite interested when a military chaplain said that he was ordered to teach troops a course on how to pick a spouse. The title of the class was "How to Avoid Marrying a Jerk". Soldiers are taught how to evaluate a potential mate's family background, attitudes, compatibility, experiences in previous relationships, and skills he or she would bring to the union. They are also taught how not to let their level of sexual involvement exceed their level of commitment or level of knowledge about the other person.

I believe Christian young people need similar training. While we should encourage Christians to marry Christians (see today's scripture again), that is not enough. Some Christians are not stable enough emotionally to build a healthy marriage. A person can be a Christian and be lacking in social skills and/or be deficient in basic common sense. He or she may love the Lord and may be going to heaven, yet still not be someone with whom you want to spend the rest of your life.

Another wise guideline is to marry someone who is your equal. Look for someone who is neither too far above you nor too far beneath you. Find someone who is a good match for you spiritually, mentally, physically, socially and emotionally. There are exceptions, but the exceptions do not negate the rule, they only prove it.

PRAYER THOUGHTS - Lord, give us wisdom and discernment in marriage and in all our relationships. Help us remember that being "unequally yoked" can hinder us from being all that we can be for You.

A SLOW FADE HARDENS THE HEART

SCRIPTURE READING - Hebrews 3:12-15

A Christian song says, "It's a slow fade when you give yourself away". People rarely make major course corrections in their lives suddenly and impulsively. Losing one's faith is seldom like the breaking of a dam that floods the valley below. It is more often like a leaky faucet that goes drip, drip, drip day after day.

Our pride and evil desires gradually pull us away from God if we don't bring them under His control. In other words, sin will cause us to disbelieve. Unbelief is evil, sufficient to keep us out of God's rest. Disobedience hardens one's heart toward God while faith grows when we obey Him.

Today's scripture urges us to obey God now while we still have the opportunity. There is danger of the same peril that beset the Israelites. God's Word calls for a response and people will either respond in obedience or stubbornly reject it. Disobedience can lead to falling away (apostasy) from the Living God. Protection against it is to be found in daily, mutual exhortation, (v. 13). Every day Christians should speak words of encouragement to each other. The many are responsible for the one. Every member of the Christian community should reach out to those who are weary and/or hurting lest they become strays.

PRAYER THOUGHTS - Righteous Father, please deliver us from pride and deceitful desires that war against our souls. Sanctify us that we may walk in holy submission to your will.

THE HARD SIDE OF GRACE

SCRIPTURE READING - Titus 2:11-14

Some people have the idea that preaching grace is soft-peddling the Gospel or letting people off easy. However, in our scripture for today, Paul explains that grace is practical and life-changing. It teaches us to say, "No" to the world and, "Yes" to God.

Paul told the Corinthians, "By the grace of God, I am what I am," (I Corinthians 15:10). God takes the initiative to reach out to us in love and offers a fresh start even though we are entirely unworthy. Romans 2:4 says, "God's kindness leads you toward repentance." It is the grace of God which breaks the sinner's heart.

Grace is also a paradox because it is free, as free as the wind, but grace is also costly. If you accept God's grace, it will cost you your very life. This is the hard side of grace. The hymn entitled "When I Survey the Wondrous Cross" contains a line which explains this hard side of grace. It says, "Love so amazing, so divine, demands my life, my soul, my all."

When we understand grace, it makes us humble. We realize that we cannot save ourselves. If we are wise, we accept the gift of salvation and become God's grateful servants.

PRAYER THOUGHTS - Gracious Father, we can never repay You for the gift of salvation purchased by the blood of Your Son. Strengthen us to be witnesses of this Good News to a lost and dying world.

THE BENEFITS OF SUFFERING

SCRIPTURE READING - James 1:2-4

C. S. Lewis said, "God whispers to us in our joy, but shouts to us in our pain." God gives us something in our pain that He cannot give us in our ease. James mentions two benefits of trials in our scripture for today—perseverance and maturity. These are great blessings, but they do not come without adversity.

This reminds me of an event which took place in my childhood. One spring when I was about ten years old, my father and I were looking at some young trees which had been planted a year earlier. All of them had leaves except one. I asked, "Did this one die during the winter?"

Dad replied, "Maybe, maybe not, let's scare it and find out."

I thought he was joking, so I laughed. But he was serious. He wrapped his hand around the trunk of the tree just below the branches. He bent it over so far I feared he would break it in two. He shook it and twisted it. While he did all that, he explained, "Sometimes during the winter the sap gets stuck in the trunk and you need to loosen it up. It's called 'scaring your tree'."

Sure enough, in a couple of days, the little tree budded and began to leaf out. Today, it is a large and beautiful shade tree. And it occurs to me that sometimes God needs to scare us just to get the spiritual sap flowing in us again. The process may be unpleasant, but if we become more fruitful, God's wisdom is once again vindicated. However, if trials fail to help us grow, it is not God's fault.

PRAYER THOUGHTS - Lord, thank you for loving us enough to allow us to experience testing. Help us to become better rather than bitter as we trust you in life's trials.

REJOICE IN THE LORD

SCRIPTURE READING - John 15:9-11

If you can start the day without caffeine or pep pills;
If you can be cheerful, ignoring aches and pains;
If you can eat the same food every day and be grateful for it;
If you can understand when loved ones are too busy to give
you time;
If you can overlook when people take things out on you—
When, through no fault of yours, something goes wrong;
If you can take criticism and blame without resentment;
If you can conquer tension without medical help;
If you can sleep without the aid of drugs;
If you can do all these things,
Then you are probably the family dog.
—Author Unknown

None of us enjoy the irritations and annoyances of life. Sometimes we as Christians find it difficult to accept when things are not going well. After all, doesn't God want His children to be happy?

Some scripture promises certainly give us that impression. For example, Psalm 37:4 says, "Delight yourself in the Lord and He will give you the desires of your heart."

For years I have read my own selfishness into that verse. I thought that if I loved and sought after God, He promised me many of the goodies of this life that I desired. But that is not what God is saying at all. He says that if we want a deep, personal relationship with Him more than anything else, it will be granted us.

That makes more sense, doesn't it? After all, what is more valuable, meaningful, and fulfilling in life than an intimate relationship with the one true and living God?

PRAYER THOUGHTS - Lord, may our heart's desire be to walk in unbroken fellowship with you. Forgive us when we stray and renew us in your love.

MAKING THE MOST OF DOWN TIME

SCRIPTURE READING - Psalm 23

Entire books have been written based on Psalm 23, it being rich with guidance and meaning. For now, let's focus on one phrase, "He makes me lie down in green pastures".

A friend who was having health problems said to me, "I don't have time for this." Nevertheless, God sometimes "makes us lie down," just as the shepherd does his sheep. Why would a sheep not want to lie down? Why would he have to be made to do so? For the same reason we sometimes need to have the reins pulled in on ourselves. Have you ever been so busy driving your car that you forgot to stop for gas? The same thing happens to us spiritually and emotionally.

Psalm 46:10 says, "Be still and know that I am God". When do we do that? Our culture does not prize or allow much time for solitude and quiet reflection. This is unfortunate because many societies on earth appreciate the value and need for it. Even more importantly, Jesus did. He often retreated to the mountains or out in a boat to think and pray.

Most of us need to take more time to reflect before God on where we have been and where we are going. Do not tempt God to slow you down in spite of yourself. Voluntarily pull yourself off the fast track and make time for creative solitude with the Lord.

PRAYER THOUGHTS - Father, forgive us when we get all stressed out and act like we need to control the universe. Teach us to be still and to remember that you are God, not us.

GOOD NEWS ABOUT GOD'S WRATH

SCRIPTURE READING - 2 Thessalonians 1:6-9; Revelation 6:15-17

We don't hear much preaching or teaching today about the wrath of God. Nobody wants to think about something so frightening. However, on the flip side of God's wrath is some good news.

The first positive note is that evil is temporary and goodness is eternal. Someday Satan, his angels, and those who prefer wickedness will be permanently put out of business. God's people will not have to endure any more violence, crime, abuse, immorality, or temptation.

Secondly, nobody has to be condemned with unbelievers. Jesus said in John 3:16, "For God so loved the world that He gave His only begotten Son, that whoever believes in Him shall not perish, but have everlasting life." You need not perish if you make Christ your Lord and Savior.

Finally, believers have a great purpose for living. Jesus calls us to share His message of salvation with others. We must urge people to run to the loving arms of Jesus and escape the wrath that is to come. It takes courage to warn people of God's wrath; but that blazing anger will be more terrifying on the final day than it is now. Let us sound the warning before it's too late!

PRAYER THOUGHTS - Righteous Father, we know that you are holy and cannot tolerate sin. Thank you for Your Son who bore our sins on the cross. Strengthen us to live for Jesus and to bring others to Him.

CONFESSION AT THE TABLE

SCRIPTURE READING - I Corinthians 11:27-32

The context of today's scripture is Paul rebuking the Corinthian Christians for abusing the Lord's Supper. Their minds were not focused on the meaning of the Lord's broken body and shed blood. They were under God's judgment because they were not examining their own hearts and actions. Repentance and confession of sin should be natural for us as we meet around the Lord's table.

The church this writer belongs to observes the Lord's Supper every Sunday. We believe this was the practice of the early church, (Acts 2:42; 20:7). When we commune with the Lord every week, we have a golden opportunity to examine ourselves spiritually, clear our consciences, and recommit ourselves to Him. Remembering what He did for us on the cross will keep us spiritually motivated.

Also, while recognizing His holiness, we become convicted of our own sins. As we confess those sins, we accept again the blood of Christ which cleanses us. We begin a new week with a clean slate and a deeper resolve to live for His glory.

The next time you partake of the emblems, remember the exhortation of today's scripture, "Everyone ought to examine themselves before they eat of the bread and drink of the cup," (I Corinthians 11:28).

PRAYER THOUGHTS - Lord, we thank you for giving us a celebration to commemorate your atoning death for us on the cross. Help us to use this sacred memorial as a time for confession of sin and spiritual renewal.

A MIRROR FOR YOUR SOUL

SCRIPTURE READING - James 1:22-25

James exhorts us to be doers of the Word and not hearers only. Does your lifestyle reflect your profession of faith? Jesus spoke of those who have been involved in ministry and yet Jesus will say to them, "I never knew you," (Matthew 7:22-23). Such persons are "Christian atheists". They say they believe in God, want to be saved, and even become active in the church, but live and make decisions as if God did not exist.

Our scripture today says that you deceive yourself if you think there is merit in reading the Word of God without doing what it says. But if you continue to read the Bible and live by its directions, you will be blessed by God.

James compares the Bible to a mirror. A mirror does not lie. What you see is how you really look. That explains why many avoid reading the Bible. They don't want to be responsible for what it might reveal about their spiritual condition. It would become more difficult to rationalize their sin.

Then there are those who read it because it makes them feel spiritual, even though they don't submit to its authority. They may enjoy discussing it as religious philosophy, but it doesn't have any relevance to their personal lives. Such attitudes are self-deception. This deception leads to spiritual malnutrition and death.

PRAYER THOUGHTS - Almighty God, we owe all allegiance to you as your children. May we love you not merely in word, but also in deed and in truth.

ORDER AMID CHAOS

SCRIPTURE READING - Genesis 45:1-8

One of the most painful experiences of my life was being forced to terminate a nineteen-year ministry. At the time, the situation seemed like a comedy of errors. I believe everybody felt like they were doing the right thing. In retrospect, I made some mistakes and so did others, but God caused it to work together for good.

In this world, change is inevitable. Some changes may frustrate us, grieve us, hurt us, or even challenge our faith.

Imagine how Joseph felt when his brothers sold him into slavery and when he was later put in prison for doing the right thing. Over time, Joseph saw that it was all part of a beautiful plan designed by a sovereign God. We will have the same experience if we just keep trusting the Lord.

"And we know that in all things God works for the good of those who love Him, who have been called according to His purpose," (Romans 8:28).

PRAYER THOUGHTS - Lord, increase our faith when we are tempted to doubt. Thank you for your promise that you will bless us in our trials and in spite of our failures.

ARE YOU A DISCIPLE?

SCRIPTURE READING - Luke 6:40

I do not know any Christians who begin their walk with Jesus and say, "I want to be a mediocre Christian". But I know a lot of mediocre Christians.

What happens along the way to make the fire go out? Why do some Christians take off like rockets and just keep climbing while others fizzle on the launching pad?

While each of us is responsible for our own attitude and growth, I believe we who are church leaders share some of the responsibility. Often, we do not have high enough expectations of church members or, if we do, we fail to communicate them clearly.

Several years ago I attended a leadership conference at the Southeast Christian Church in Louisville, Kentucky. The leaders of that congregation had come up with a description of a spiritually mature Christian. They called it "Six Habits of a Disciple". They are:

- Communicates regularly with God through prayer.
- Studies God's Word.
- Produces the fruit of the Spirit.
- Worships God with a church body.
- Shares Christ with others.

- Serves Christ through the giving of time, talents, and earthly treasure.

The person who lives out these habits is the type of disciple Southeast seeks to produce. They strongly encourage all new members to spend one hour per week in worship at church, one hour as a volunteer for the church, and one hour in study with God's people (Sunday School, home Bible study, or another Bible study group).

I thought these ideas were right on. What do you think and how do you measure up?

PRAYER THOUGHTS - Lord, may our obsession be to become like you. Help us to be found faithful and fruitful for your glory.

BE INTENTIONAL ABOUT PRAYER

SCRIPTURE READING - I Chronicles 16:8-11

Our scripture for today is a psalm of David. In verse eleven, he says, "Look to the Lord and his strength; seek his face always." One way we do that is through prayer.

Most of us need regular encouragement in this area because it is easy for us to forget to pray. If we miss work, our boss will want to know why. If we skip out on church, our friends will miss us. But we can go day after day without anybody, other than God, knowing that we have neglected prayer.

The fact is that most of us underestimate the importance of prayer. Did you know that twenty-five of the twenty-eight chapters in the book of Acts mention prayer? The early church turned the world upside down, in spite of great opposition, because they were people of prayer. Likewise, we will not have spiritual victory in our personal lives or in the church without the power of God unleashed through prayer. That is why the devil seeks to distract and discourage us from praying.

The only way we can overcome the inertia we feel about prayer is to be intentional about it, to see it as the necessity it is, just like food, water, and rest. As one wise person put it, "When you don't feel like praying, talk to God about it."

PRAYER THOUGHTS - Heavenly Father, please forgive us when we forget to pray. Remind us daily of the many exhortations to prayer in your Word and the promises for those who pray.

DECLARE GOD'S TRUTH

SCRIPTURE READING - Ezekiel 3:18-19

The Bible says, "Rebuke your neighbor frankly so you will not share in his guilt," (Leviticus 19:17). In other words, if we do not confront people about their sin, God holds us partly responsible for their disobedience.

The world doesn't think this way. Our society has a "live and let live" attitude. We celebrate tolerance and diversity.

This worldly attitude has sometimes spilled over into the church. In our desire to reach more people, we may be tempted to water down our teaching. The result is feel-good messages, avoiding such biblical topics as sin, repentance, judgment, hell, and God's call for holy living. Instead, people are told how to use the Bible to solve their problems and find success and happiness. The danger here is that your focus is more on the creature rather than the Creator.

Teaching the truth requires courage. More than that, it demonstrates genuine love for the hearer. God rebukes us because He loves us, just as a loving parent corrects a child. Those who are not disciplined are illegitimate, (Hebrews 12:8).

It is a myth that spiritually hungry people want to be coddled. True seekers are hungry for the truth and will be drawn to it. We cannot build up the body of Christ with junk food for the soul.

This doesn't mean that we need to be harsh or blunt. Rather, we must pray for wisdom to share the whole truth in an interesting and relevant way.

PRAYER THOUGHTS - Heavenly Father, please give us both courage and wisdom to confront others with the claims of Christ. May we never forget that the most unloving thing we can do is to keep the Good News from a friend.

CHOOSING A CHURCH

SCRIPTURE READING - Hebrews 2:10-12

What should you look for when selecting a church home? Theologically, there are four types of churches today. These may be categorized as: Cults, Catholic Churches, Liberal Churches, and Evangelical Churches.

Cults have one or more of the following characteristics: they may humanize God, deify man, minimize sin, and ostracize the Scriptures. Cults usually follow "prophets" and writings other than the Bible and regard these as superior to the Scriptures.

Catholic churches base their teachings on the Bible plus the traditions of the church. Some of their traditions contradict the Scriptures. Examples are the authority of the pope, the veneration of Mary, an exclusive priesthood, and purgatory.

Liberal churches do not wear that name per se, such as "First Liberal Church". But many denominations fall into this category. Their teaching is based on the Bible plus human reason. If there is a contradiction between the two, they go with human reason. As a result, they reject the supernatural in Scripture (such as the miracles of Jesus). This approach undermines both the deity of Christ and the authority of the Bible.

The fourth type of church is the category closest to what this writer believes. These are the Evangelical churches. Such groups believe that the Bible is fully-inspired of God and is our all-sufficient guide in matters of faith and practice. We believe that God created the earth, that Jesus was born of a virgin, died on the cross for our sins, rose bodily from the tomb, ascended into heaven, and is coming back for those who love Him. We believe that salvation is found only in Christ (Acts 4:12), and are dedicated to sharing that message with the world. (One caution here: Not all churches that wear the name "Evangelical" are evangelical.)

PRAYER THOUGHTS - Lord, we thank you for the church which is your Body on earth. May we be true to your Word and faithful to your mission of sharing the Gospel with all nations.

RESTORING THE NEW
TESTAMENT CHURCH

SCRIPTURE READING - Ephesians 2:17-22

The churches I have belonged to and ministered with all my life are part of the Restoration Movement which began on the American frontier early in the nineteenth century. It was begun by Christians who were tired of denominationalism and Catholicism and decided to go back to the simple faith and doctrine of the church revealed in the New Testament. Following are seven principles which came out of that movement.

The Bible is our only rule of faith and practice, (2 Timothy 3:16-17).

The restoration of the church of the New Testament in all of its essentials, (Ephesians 2:19-20)

A proper distinction between the Old and New Testaments - The Law was local and temporary but the Gospel is universal and for all time, (Hebrews 8:6-7, 13).

The autonomy of the local church - We renounce the authority of all ecclesiastical governing bodies outside of the local church, (Acts 14:23, Titus 1:5).

We recognize that Christ is the head over all things to the church and has delegated His authority to no man or group of men, (Ephesians 1:22-23).

We believe in the restoration of the ordinances of Christ (baptism and the Lord's Supper) to their original meaning and place, (Acts 2:38, 42; 20:7; 22:16, Matthew 26:26-29, I Corinthians 11:23-29).

Our plea is the unity of all believers based upon the essentials of the faith, (John 17:20-21).

It is hard to improve on just following the Bible as the path to Christian unity. May this be our strategy so the Lord may be glorified in His Church!

PRAYER THOUGHTS - Lord, forgive us when we exalt our opinions or traditions above Your Word. Help us to be faithful to the pattern revealed for the church by the New Testament apostles and prophets.

WHY IS JESUS THE ONLY WAY?

SCRIPTURE READING - John 14:1-6

A Christian missionary was asked, "Why do the Japanese people need Christ when they already have Confucius?" The missionary replied, "Three reasons:

- Confucius was a teacher, but Jesus is a Savior.
- Confucius is dead, while Jesus is alive.
- Jesus will someday judge Confucius, you, me and everybody."

This missionary's answer is similar to the answer I give when somebody asks me, "Why is Jesus the only way?" I reply that Jesus is the only founder of any major world religion who claimed to be God. Then I ask, "Who else in all of history lived without sin, yet died for your sins? Who else in history laid down his life for you and three days later took it back again?" Finally I ask, "To whom else will you turn for the forgiveness of sins and the gift of eternal life?"

Sometimes people say, "Isn't it rather arrogant to say that Jesus is the only way?" However, the fact is that all religions make truth claims. Muslims claim that Mohammed is the prophet we should listen to. Hindus make truth claims about reincarnation and karma. Buddhism began because Buddha disagreed with some of the truth claims of Hinduism.

The bottom line is that each of us ought to examine the witnesses and evidence for each religion. Then we can decide if any of them has the ring of truth.

PRAYER THOUGHTS - Gracious Father, we thank You for making a way for us to reach You through Your Son and our Savior Jesus Christ. Give us holy boldness to be His witnesses in a sometimes hostile world.

WISE USE OF TIME AND PEOPLE

SCRIPTURE READING - Exodus 18:13-26

All of us have had the experience of saying something which seemed intelligent at the time, but after proper reflection we realized it made no sense. For example, in 1975, Sylvia and I went on a trip with my parents. On the way home, my mother was talking about all the things she had to do when we got back. I could see that Dad was tired of hearing her litany because he was on vacation and wanted to relax. Finally he said, "Mary, if you did everything you were supposed to do, you'd never get anything done." All of us thought about what he had said for a few seconds, and then burst out laughing.

I was reminded of that incident recently when I read the following statement by Frank Rizzo, ex-police chief and mayor of Philadelphia. He said, "The streets are safe in Philadelphia; it's only the people who make them unsafe."

Now, we can figure out what Dad and Rizzo were trying to say. Dad meant to say that we need to do the important things first or we will just fritter away our time. Rizzo was saying that good streets are useless if they are overrun by bad people. In other words, using our time wisely and developing good people are crucial.

As Moses learned in our text, you will burn out if you attempt to do everything by yourself. Don't try to do the work of ten people, get ten people to do the work.

PRAYER THOUGHTS - Lord, give us wisdom to focus on our highest priorities and then help us to enlist others for projects which will honor you.

HOW TO RESIST TEMPTATION

SCRIPTURE READING - James 4:4-10

Life is full of pitfalls and temptations and trials. The Bible warns us that the devil is real and dangerous, but God's Word assures us that we can overcome temptation and stand against other attacks of the evil one.

Victory over sin and discouragement begins with surrender to God. "The fear of God is the beginning of wisdom," (Proverbs 1:7). We do not fear God because He is out to get us, but because we are ultimately accountable to Him and our fate is in His hands. This should motivate us to respect God and His Word.

We not only revere Him for who He is, but should love and trust Him because of what He has done for us in Christ. So James exhorts us to "submit to God first," then we have the power to "resist the devil" and he will back off.

God also expects us to use our consecrated common sense. We need to be aware of our personal weaknesses and avoid people, places and situations that tempt us. If you do not want to enter the devil's house, stay off his front porch.

God promises to provide "a way of escape" when we are tempted (I Corinthians 10:13), but we must prayerfully and sincerely want it and seek it.

PRAYER THOUGHTS - Righteous Father, we thank you that victory over Satan and sin is available from your hand. Give us grace to tap into your power every day.

CHURCH DISCIPLINE

SCRIPTURE READING - I Corinthians 5:1-13

The world often has a "live-and-let-live" attitude toward sin, but the church must take it seriously when there is sin among its members. There is no such thing as private sin in the body of Christ. When a Christian refuses to repent, it affects the entire church.

The Bible says that the church must enforce consequences for unrepentant sin. Jesus talked about it in Matthew 18:15-19 and so did Paul in our scripture for today.

One thing that may keep us from obeying these commands is that such discipline may seem mean-spirited. But discipline should be seen as a positive thing. No discipline seems pleasant at the time to those being disciplined, (Hebrews 12:11). However, its purpose is positive, to bring people back to fellowship with God and His people, (2 Corinthians 2:6-8).

We fear ruffling anyone's feathers by holding them accountable. This is a mistake. We have too many homes, too many schools, and too many churches where there are no consequences. If we simply do what the Lord has told us to do, we will get what the Lord wants us to have.

PRAYER THOUGHTS - Dear God, please give us the courage to do the hard things you ask us to do. Help us to remember that a rebel's heart can be softened by loving and firm discipline.

THE IMPORTANCE OF MOTIVATION

SCRIPTURE READING - Colossians 3:23-25

Proverbs 19:15 says, "Laziness brings on deep sleep, and the shiftless go hungry". The book of Proverbs has a lot to say about the need for diligence and the folly of slothfulness. Motivation is usually the difference between success or failure in any enterprise.

One Sunday after preaching on motivation, a sharp senior citizen handed me a note and said, "I'm very interested in motivation." His note had four words on it that caught my attention. They all began with the letter "P". Here they are:

1. PRAISE - Do not expect people to praise you. You must learn to be a self-starter. Be proactive, which means that you accept responsibility for your life. Get the best education you can and put it to work.

2. PRIDE - Pride can be negative, but there is also a healthy pride. We should not think of ourselves as being better than others, but we can feel good about ourselves when we have done our very best.

3. POWER - Power alone will not win the race. There is a difference between power and authority. Jesus became most powerless when he surrendered himself to the cross but through that act he gained for himself incredible authority. Jesus taught that greatness is found in

service to God and others, not by "throwing our weight around".

4. POOR - Being poor can be a problem, but being rich is not the answer. If money is your goal, you will never be satisfied. Be a life-long learner, work hard, learn how to manage your money and be fair with God and He will take care of your needs.

PRAYER THOUGHTS - Father, teach us those things which please You and then inspire us with zeal for Your Kingdom.

SEEK HUMILITY

SCRIPTURE READING - Matthew 18:1-4

These are strong words from Jesus. Unless we humble ourselves like a little child, we will never enter God's Kingdom. The Lord did not tell children to receive the faith as adults, he said to adults that they are to receive the faith like a child. Little children are dependent, obedient, and teachable. Unless we emulate these qualities, we are useless to God.

We also need to cultivate a spirit of humility in our relationships with others. Paul said in Ephesians 4:2, "Be completely humble and gentle; be patient, bearing with one another in love."

We not only need God, we desperately need others if we are to thrive spiritually. Pride separates us from God and others. Humility opens the door.

We do not become humble by downgrading ourselves, but by seeing ourselves realistically through the eyes of God. We can and should be both humble and courageous. Humility is confidence properly placed. As Christians, we are empowered by the Holy Spirit. Ephesians 6:10 says, "Be strong in the Lord and in the power of his might." Let us seek the holy boldness that comes as we humble ourselves before God!

PRAYER THOUGHTS - Sovereign Lord, may we not think of ourselves more highly than we ought, but help us to realize all we can do by abiding in You.

WATCH YOUR TONGUE

SCRIPTURE READING - Matthew 12:36-37

Jesus' words in our scripture reading are sobering to one like myself who enjoys joking around. God takes our words seriously. James 1:26 says, "Those who consider themselves religious and yet do not keep a tight rein on their tongues deceive themselves and their religion is worthless."

Only human beings, of all God's earthly creations, have the gift of speech. This is one way we are, "created in God's image," (Genesis 1:26-27). God is grieved when we use our words to tear others down rather than to build them up. If your tongue is out of control, you are fooling yourself if you believe your spiritual life is healthy.

Ephesians 4:15 tells us to speak the truth in love. Even if we must correct somebody, we should make sure they know we love them and are not out to get them and, of course, slander and gossip should have no place in the mouth of a Christian. I like to compare slander and gossip to a gun and the words we speak are bullets. Such bullets can cause great harm and even death. Once the bullet comes out of the gun, you can't change your mind and take it back.

We are never to use our tongues to put others down. Instead, we are to edify each other in what we say and thereby bless those who hear us, (Ephesians 4:29).

PRAYER THOUGHTS - Lord Jesus, please sanctify our speech in self-control. May our words encourage and strengthen others that you may be glorified in us.

HAVE YOU REPENTED?

SCRIPTURE READING - Isaiah 55:6-7

Comedian Red Green often closed his TV show with this so-called "Man Prayer": "I'm a man. I can change if I want to, I guess." He did this for a laugh, but have you noticed how often good humor mirrors real life? This half-hearted commitment to make necessary changes unmasks our own hypocrisy. When we confess our sins to God, knowing that it is just a matter of time before we repeat the same offense, this sows seeds of apostasy.

Apostasy means to fall away from God. This happened to Cain in the fourth chapter of Genesis. Because his faith in God was defective, the Lord rejected Cain's offering. When God accepted the offering of his brother, Cain reacted with jealousy and took his brother's life. Before he did that however, God gave him a chance to do the right thing. Genesis 4:6-7 says, "Then the Lord said to Cain, 'Why are you angry? Why is your face downcast? If you do what is right, will you not be accepted? But if you do not do what is right, sin is crouching at your door; it desires to have you, but you must master it.'"

As soon as we are convicted of our sin, we must resolve to renounce it and change. This is repentance. To repent means to change both our mind and our actions to conform to God's will.

Paul summed up his preaching in Acts 26:20. He says that he told every-body, "they should repent and turn to God and prove their repentance by their deeds." We ought to preach the same message and then practice what we preach.

PRAYER THOUGHTS - Father, our heart's desire is to please you. Give us strength to change our hearts when we are tempted to please ourselves or others.

UNDERSTANDING FORGIVENESS

SCRIPTURE READING - Ephesians 4:31-32

During my years of ministry, one of the most frequently asked questions has been, "What does it mean to forgive those who do me wrong?" This is especially difficult if the person who offended us is not sorry. In other words, must we forgive others even if they are unrepentant?

Obviously, God does not expect us to do more than He Himself is willing to do. God does not forgive His enemies unconditionally. The difference between God and us, however, is that we are commanded not to get revenge, but to turn our enemies over to God for retribution, (Romans 12:19).

We are also commanded to be willing to forgive (see today's scripture) and to love and pray for our enemies, (Matthew 5:43-48). Furthermore, scriptures such as Proverbs 25:21-22 and Romans 12:20 exhort us to do good to our enemies. If an offender is unrepentant then full reconciliation may never be possible. Even if offenders acknowledge their sin, it may take time to rebuild our trust in them, but we should still forgive.

Motivation to forgive is important. We forgive for others' sake so they will taste God's unmerited mercy. We forgive for our own sake so we will be free from the burden of bitterness. Most of all, we forgive for the Lord's sake to honor Him, thank Him and imitate Him. Forgiveness cost Jesus the cross and that is a price we could never match.

PRAYER THOUGHTS - Gracious Lord, great is Your mercy toward us. Give us strength to extend mercy to others.

MAKING YOUR ROUTINE SACRED

SCRIPTURE READING - Colossians 3:22-24

Our text for today says that even the work of a slave is sacramental if it is done to praise God and not merely for human approval. In another place Paul the apostle says, "So whether you eat or drink or whatever you do, do it all for the glory of God," (I Corinthians 10:31).

The natural tendency is for us to compartmentalize our lives between the sacred and the secular. Prayer, reading the Bible, going to church, and so on are considered sacred activities. The things we do to make a living, get an education, and meet our physical needs are considered secular. God's Word, however, makes no such distinction.

If we have been born again and seek to please God in all we do, every act of life becomes sacred. Some have taught that we are more spiritual if we forbid people to marry or eat meat, for example. The Bible calls such thinking demonic. All things God has created are to be enjoyed by believers and are consecrated. They are to be received with thanksgiving and prayer, (I Timothy 4:1-5).

PRAYER THOUGHTS - Creator God, we thank You for the gift of life. Help us to bring glory to You in all that we do.

WORSHIP GOD WITH JOYFUL SONGS

SCRIPTURE READING - Psalm 100

Music is a natural medium for expressing both convictions and emotions. Therefore, it is not surprising that singing became a normal component in worship. People have different tastes in music. Perhaps that is why the Bible advocates using a variety of musical styles.

Ephesians 5:19 says that we should worship using "psalms, hymns and spiritual songs". Psalms are scripture set to music, Hymns are Christian poetry that is sung while spiritual songs refer to shorter poems that were sung using popular melodies of the day (tunes used in places of amusement and the theater).

God loves variety and we should worship Him that way. Some lyrics are meat while others are milk. Some music reaches the head while other songs touch the heart. Our worship will be more balanced if we seek a beautiful blend of all.

PRAYER THOUGHTS - Lord, we thank you for the gift of music. Above all, we thank you for glorious good news to sing about. Help us to use this medium to reach the lost and edify the saved.

FINISH WELL

SCRIPTURE READING - Psalm 92:12-15

Getting older is sometimes difficult. My wife and I were reminded of this when our daughter was in nursing school. Katie came home for spring break. Sylvia and I were talking about being in our fifties and Katie said, "In one of my classes we're learning about people your age."

I asked her, "What are you learning?"

She replied, "In your fifties is when things start to wear out."

I had to admit at that point that some of my body parts were not working as well as they had a few years earlier. However, now that I'm in my sixties, the body I had at age fifty looks pretty good. One lady who was nearing her sixtieth birthday said, "It didn't bother me turning forty or even fifty, but sixty is the worst. I'll really be old."

What about this age thing anyway? Here is how I see it. According to the life expectancy charts, I have now lived about 85% of the normal life span. That means I'm in the "home stretch". If heaven awaits me at the end of my earthly pilgrimage, then I ought to be more joyful now than when I was a young man. I am this much nearer my goal!

When we cling to this life like the world does, our lives become a standing contradiction of the faith we profess. Young people need to see hope in the eyes of we who are older, not doubt and despair. God has promised His children that the best is yet to come!

PRAYER THOUGHTS - Lord, keep our faith strong at the end so we do not ruin our testimony. Help us to finish well!

LIVING BY FAITH

SCRIPTURE READING - Matthew 6:25-34

What is faith, anyway? Faith is a combination of risk and commitment. God calls us to live by faith, (Romans 1:17).

The first element of faith is risk. If you already have the money in the bank, it's not faith. If you can see how you can make it happen, it's not faith. If your goal is so small you can do it without God, you don't need faith. Faith means going where God leads even if it looks impossible.

But faith not only involves risk, it requires commitment. I do not know who wrote the following words, but they can change your life. They were written under the heading "Commitment is the Key".

"Until I am committed, there is hesitancy, a chance to draw back. But the moment I definitely commit myself, then God begins to move also, and a whole stream of events begins to erupt. All manner of unforeseen incidents, meetings, persons and material assistance that I could never have dreamed would come my way, begin to flow toward me the moment I make a commitment."

The problem is that most people want resources to flow to them without them taking a stand and making a commitment. They say, "God, just take care of me and I'll serve you."

But God says, "No, you just serve me and I will take care of you."

Or they say, "Just bless me and I'll obey you."

And He says, "No, you obey me and then I will bless you."

Let's not spiritually get the cart before the horse in our daily Christian lives. There is nothing more rewarding than living by faith in Christ.

PRAYER THOUGHTS - Lord, we thank you for the promise of your care as we seek first your Kingdom. Strengthen our faith that we may claim your promises.

PRAYER AND FASTING

SCRIPTURE READING - Matthew 6:16-18

A lady told about a beggar who came to her door and asked for something to eat. She said that she was preparing dinner and would bring him out a plate of food. He thanked her, but she said, "Don't thank me. Do you see that pile of wood out there?"

He lied and said, "No."

She said, "I saw you see it".

He replied, "I know you saw me see it, but you won't see me saw it."

There are many freeloaders in this world, but each of us is called to servanthood in the Kingdom of God. A big part of being useful to God is learning to listen to His voice. One biblical way of doing that is through prayer and fasting.

Fasting is not a popular spiritual discipline in our affluent American culture. Jesus gave directions about this practice in the Sermon on the Mount. In our scripture for today, Jesus said, "When you fast…" (Matthew 6:16). He did not say, "If you fast…" Fasting is something he assumed we would do. In fasting, we skip one or more meals. We spend the time we would ordinarily use to prepare and consume food to pray instead.

Prayer and fasting is just another way of listening to God's voice. This writer has been practicing prayer and fasting nearly every week for several years and I recommend it. If your health will not permit you to skip a meal, you can give up something else to make more time for God. Jesus promised that if we fast and pray quietly and humbly, the Father will reward us, (Matthew 6:18).

PRAYER THOUGHTS - Heavenly Father, we thank You that You love us and desire intimate fellowship with each of us. May we use every means at our disposal to draw close to You and to seek Your face in our daily lives.

REAL CHURCH GROWTH

SCRIPTURE READING - Acts 2:38-42

Most churches want to grow. Unfortunately, many see church growth as "anything for the sake of numbers". But the biblical idea of church growth is that the new converts are to be nurtured and incorporated into the life of the church. When those who are led to Christ maintain a lifelong relationship with the church, growth is the result. Such growth is both numerical and spiritual.

There is nothing wrong with numerical growth. Our Lord seemed to be very much concerned with numbers. The fish in the miraculous catch were counted, the leftovers after the feeding of the five thousand were counted, and the five thousand themselves were counted! Converts at Pentecost were counted. In the parable of the lost sheep, the shepherd would never have known that one of his flock of one hundred was lost unless he had counted them!

The point we need to keep in mind is that we are seeking to make disciples, not just looking for decisions. In order to do that, our passion must be for those who are yet outside of Christ and His church. We must prefer to seek the lost rather than satisfy the saved. Those who are saved must be taught to sacrifice their preferences, when necessary, for the sake of our mission—reaching and teaching the lost!

PRAYER THOUGHTS - Father, help us to be like our Savior who came to seek and to save the lost. May we never forget that those who are baptized into Christ must be taught to obey His commands.

HEARING GOD'S CALL

SCRIPTURE READING - I Samuel 3:1-14

What constitutes a call from God? How do we know when God is giving us a specific task to perform? God called Moses from a burning bush. Jesus called Paul out of a blinding light. Most of us, however, are guided by the Spirit in less dramatic ways.

One of my seminary professors said that Need + Opportunity = A Call from God. Often the Lord's call is just that simple.

In today's scripture, Samuel was confused about who was calling him because he "did not yet know the Lord," (vs. 7). We need to pray that we will learn how to listen to God's voice.

God guides us through such things as the Scriptures, prayer, wise counsel from others, and the trend of circumstances. Sometimes God gives us multiple choices. He says, in effect, "A, B, C or D, any one is fine with me." At other times, He gives us a clear call to a specific choice or mission.

God may give you an assignment that seems risky or even dangerous. Keep in mind, however, that the safest place to be is wherever God wants you to be. Wherever He guides, He will provide, (Philippians 4:19).

PRAYER THOUGHTS - Lord, give us patience to wait for your leading and give us peace when we are on the right path.

MUST I BE IMMERSED?

SCRIPTURE READING - Hebrews 10:19-23

A religious phenomenon of the 1990s was that for the first time in America more than half of Protestants belonged to churches which baptize by immersion. This occurred because many main-line denominations which sprinkle or pour declined in membership. At the same time, the independent and conservative evangelical churches which immerse experienced significant growth.

It is not difficult to understand why those who believe the Bible means what it says prefer immersion. You do not have to know Greek to understand that baptize means "to immerse". A cursory look at the English Bible clearly reveals that first century baptism was by immersion.

For example, John 3:23 tells us that John the Baptist, "baptized at Aenon near Salem because there was much water there". After Jesus was baptized, the Bible says, "he came up out of the water," (Matthew 3:16). When Philip baptized the Ethiopian eunuch, they both, "went down into the water," (Acts 8:38). Romans 6:4 compares baptism to a burial. I Peter 3:21 says that baptism saves us not because it washes dirt from the body, but because we are committing ourselves to God.

Sometimes people ask me, "What about those who are sprinkled? How will God deal with them?" All I can say is, "I don't know." I do know that when it comes to baptism, you cannot do any more than be immersed. So why do less and take a chance?

PRAYER THOUGHTS - Heavenly Father, we thank you that when we are baptized by immersion into Christ, we can also portray His death, burial, and resurrection by which we are saved.

TAKE YOUR MARRIAGE SERIOUSLY

SCRIPTURE READING - Genesis 2:20-24

One of my roles during forty-five years of ministry was helping couples with troubled marriages. Here is a typical scenario which I saw played out many times.

A married person contacts me (in the majority of cases, it was the wife). She and her husband are having problems. She describes the situation and asks me what I think. I say, "You and your husband need to sit down with someone who is able to help you evaluate your marriage and come up with a game plan to improve your relationship."

At this point, the wife's eyes fill with tears. She says, "My husband would never agree to that. He thinks counselors only stir up trouble. He says we can fix the problem ourselves, but I know we can't. We're in a rut and can't get out."

Unfortunately, she is usually right. She tells her husband what I have said, but he won't listen. Six months later, the husband stops by my office, a broken man. His wife is talking to a lawyer about getting a divorce. He asks, "Will you talk to her about reconsidering her decision?" I try, but it is usually too late. She is now the one who refuses to talk. She is burned out and has given up.

You may think your marriage is fine, but if your spouse is unhappy, you have marriage problems. Take it seriously. Don't be afraid to ask for help. The

Bible tells us that marriage is our most important human relationship, second only to our relationship with God.

PRAYER THOUGHTS - Dear God, we thank you for healthy marriages and strong homes which are basic to a functional society. Give us wisdom to take marriage as seriously as You do.

GOALS PRECEDE ACHIEVEMENT

SCRIPTURE READING - James 4:13-17

Some have misunderstood our scripture for today. They interpret it to mean that it is evil to set goals. But James is not condemning the making of plans prayerfully to the glory of God. He is rather exhorting us not to boast about what we plan to do.

We must seek God's will for the future and make our plans accordingly. Such goals are not carnal, they are merely statements of what we intend to do for God. Good goals provide structure, motivation, and accountability.

Nothing much gets done unless you first pray about it, picture it in your mind, and have a method by which to measure your progress. Once you know where you intend to go, you can invite others to join you on the journey. This will multiply your efforts.

The greatest leaders in the Bible were goal-oriented individuals. Moses tried to liberate his people forty years before God called him to do so. David wrote songs to worship God long before he laid the plans for God's temple. Paul was zealous for the Kingdom of God for years before he discovered he was supporting it from the wrong side. Our Lord Himself "set His face like a flint toward Jerusalem".

What is God calling you to do? Pray, plan, and passionately pursue those goals!

PRAYER THOUGHTS - Dear God, You have promised that when we ask in faith, You will give us wisdom. Please guide us as we seek your direction, make plans, and set goals.

REST FOR YOUR SOUL

SCRIPTURE READING - Matthew 11:28-30

A friend of mine, who is in a people-helping profession, boasted that he had not taken a vacation in over twenty years. Not long after that he developed health problems which the doctor said were stress-related. He missed eleven months of work in order to get his health back. He told me, "I have learned the hard way that if I don't take a vacation, my body will take one on its own."

Clovis Chappel, one of the great preachers of the twentieth century, said, "The most religious thing a tired Christian can do is rest." During a busy period of his ministry, Jesus told his disciples, "Come with me to a quiet place and get some rest," (Mark 6:31). That sounds like biblical justification for a vacation, doesn't it?

I don't know about you, but when I get tired, I also get negative. That is a luxury I cannot afford in ministry. One Christian lady asked her pastor, "When are you going to take some time off?"

He replied, "The devil doesn't take a vacation, so why should I?"

She wisely responded, "If you don't take a vacation, you will start to resemble the devil in other ways."

Ultimately, the best rest is available to us on a daily basis whether we are on vacation or not. In our scripture for today, Jesus said, "Come to me all you who are weary and burdened and I will give you rest." He was speaking of rest for our souls or spiritual rest. Have you found that rest in Jesus?

PRAYER THOUGHTS - Dear Lord, thank you for being our refuge in times of trouble and the Shepherd of our souls. Strengthen us today so that we will not become weary in doing good.

FEELING GOOD ABOUT FEELING BAD

SCRIPTURE READING - Romans 7:21-25

In our Bible reading today, Paul tells of the struggle between his flesh and the Spirit of God within him. It is a paradox that in order to be saved we must own our sin and disown our sin at the same time. Jesus Christ delivers us from the power and the penalty of sin, but we still struggle with the pull of sin in numerous ways.

Paul says in Galatians 5:16, "...live by the Spirit, and you will not gratify the desires of the sinful nature". Notice, Paul doesn't say we will not have sinful desires. He says, however, that we must choose not to gratify those desires.

This reminds me of a conversation I had with a lady whose husband had left her for another woman. She said, "I must be a terrible person because I keep thinking of things I can do to get even with them."

I replied, "What do you do with those ideas when they pop into your head?"

She said, "Oh, I dismiss them because I know they are wrong and vengeful."

Then I told her, "You shouldn't feel guilty then. You are being tempted to sin, but you are saying 'No' to the temptations." I continued, "There is nothing sinful about being tempted. Even Jesus was tempted, but He did not sin."

Paul and this woman were feeling bad about their sinful nature. We will too if our hearts are right. But we can feel good because God gives us the power to say "No," and if we mess up, we can confess our sin and be forgiven through Christ, (I John 1:9).

PRAYER THOUGHTS - Lord, we sometimes feel guilty about being human. Remind us of our new nature in Christ and help us claim the Spirit's power that we may overcome temptation.

IS JESUS YOUR KING?

SCRIPTURE READING - Luke 14:25-33

Many people followed Jesus as admirers and believed he was the Messiah, but they did not understand the nature of his kingdom. In today's text the Lord urges would-be followers to count the cost of discipleship. Being his disciple requires taking up his cross after him. It means renouncing everything we have and putting him first. It means living in a self-sacrificial way for the sake of his kingdom.

Jesus promises his followers abundant life in this world and eternal life in the age to come, but these benefits require commitment on our part. Many want Jesus to be their Savior, Redeemer and friend, but are unwilling to make him their Lord, Master, and King.

The Bible describes Jesus as both our Savior and Lord. However, it calls him "Savior" no more than eighteen times while he is called "Lord" more than five hundred times. Obviously, the Holy Spirit knew we would have trouble remembering that Jesus is Lord.

While following Jesus is costly, it is still the best bargain in the universe. Paul said, "For to me to live is Christ and to die is gain," (Philippians 1:21). If you live for money, to die is loss. If you live for pleasure, to die is loss. If you live for family, to die is loss. But if you live for Christ, to die is gain.

PRAYER THOUGHTS   King Jesus, as you put us first on the cross, help us to put you first in this life, that we may reign with you in glory.

HOW TO KNOW GOD'S WILL

SCRIPTURE READING - Judges 6:36-40

One of the questions I have been most frequently asked is, "How can I know God's will in this or that situation?" Gideon in our text laid out a fleece to determine God's will. Is this a good way for us to obtain divine guidance?

Gideon asked for a miracle. Do we have the right to ask that of God? The truth is that Gideon was an unusual case. God had already called him in a miraculous way, sending an angel to inform him of God's will, so he had a precedent for dealing in the miraculous. We do not.

The fact is that God guides most of us in less spectacular ways. We should always consult the Bible for wise counsel and also pray for the Lord to direct us. James 1:5-8 assures us of God's wisdom if we ask for it in faith. God also often shows us the way through the advice of other people of faith. Jesus taught us to "ask, seek and knock," (Matthew 7:7). The Apostle Paul often spoke of the Lord opening and closing doors, but we still need to be knocking on those doors.

Sometimes we get too anxious and run ahead of God. If I do not wait for the Lord to reveal His will, I usually regret it later. Don't barge ahead until you have peace that God is in it. If you are prayerfully seeking God's will, He will give you peace if you are going in the right direction, (Philippians 4:6-7).

PRAYER THOUGHTS - Lord, please keep us from making harmful choices and draw us back when we stray from the "straight and narrow".

GET SERIOUS ABOUT SIN

SCRIPTURE READING - Psalm 51:7-13

The closer we get to God, the more sensitive we are to sin in our lives. Most of us take sin too lightly. I John 2:4 says, "The man who says, 'I know him,' but does not do what he commands is a liar, and the truth is not in him."

As a young man, I went through a period when I was not as close to God as I should have been. One night during that time, I was driving in my car and listening to a sermon on the radio by evangelist Billy Graham. He said something that shook me out of my spiritual lethargy. He said, "Every sin we commit, even though we may be forgiven, makes us less effective for God than we otherwise might have been."

I had never thought of that before. I figured if I mess up, I can ask God to forgive me and I'd be as good as new. But the reality is that my testimony had been weakened, precious time had been wasted, and my spiritual growth had been interrupted. When we take one of the Devil's detours, we can never catch up to what we might have been and done for the Lord.

God spoke through the prophet Isaiah, "Surely the arm of the Lord is not too short to save, nor His ear too dull to hear. But your iniquities have separated you from your God; your sins have hidden His face from you, so that He will not hear," (Isaiah 59:1-2).

Is there some sin for which you need to repent? It behooves each of us to examine ourselves in this matter.

PRAYER THOUGHTS - Gracious Father, thank you for your patience with our going astray. Give us a godly sorrow over our sins that will lead us to repentance.

FOR MEN ONLY

SCRIPTURE READING - Proverbs 5

It is no accident that one of the biblical qualifications for church leadership is being "a one-woman man". If a man won't keep his wedding vows, he cannot be trusted to keep any of his commitments.

What does it take to be a "one-woman man"? Here are some suggestions:

Be faithful to your wife in your THOUGHTS. Jesus taught that adultery begins with lust. No lust - no adultery.

Be a one-woman man with your EYES. For example, you sometimes cannot avoid seeing a woman who is immodestly clad but you don't have to take a second look. Also, avoid pornography or anything that stirs up tainted thoughts.

Then be a one-woman man with your HANDS. A man's hands are part of his sexual equipment. Do not use your hands with a woman other than your wife in such a way as to transmit a seductive signal.

Be faithful with your LIPS. Be careful what you say to women. Do not tell suggestive stories or flirt.

Finally, be a one-woman man with your FEET. If you find that another woman tempts you, steer clear of her. Men and boys should study our scripture for today. The fifth chapter of Proverbs gives good advice on how to escape the snares of adultery.

PRAYER THOUGHTS - Lord, give us the self-discipline to set boundaries and show integrity in our relationships with the opposite sex.

THE DANGER OF SELF-RIGHTEOUSNESS

SCRIPTURE READING - Luke 18:9-14

This parable of Jesus reveals the obvious ugliness of self-righteousness. However, it is always easier to spot a self-righteous attitude in others than to see it in ourselves. We all have blind spots. We are in some ways unmerciful, unloving, unteachable and unsanctified. We don't see them because they are, well, blind spots.

That is why we need to be daily into God's Word. James calls the Bible a mirror for our souls, (1:23-25). It shows us our real spiritual condition. It convicts us of changes we need to make, (Hebrews 4:12).

But Bible knowledge is not enough by itself. The scribes and Pharisees knew the Scriptures very well. Jesus, however, was calling people into a relationship with himself that would connect us with God. Law without relationship leads to rebellion. Religion without relationship focuses on human goodness. We do righteous deeds to impress God. Instead, we must learn to be impressed by the Lord and respond to his divine person and call. We are saved and then sanctified, not vice versa.

PRAYER THOUGHTS - Righteous Father, forgive us for our religious pride. Help us to see Jesus that we may realize our spiritual poverty apart from Him.

THE ABC's OF SALVATION

SCRIPTURE READING - Acts 2:36-41

Have you ever accepted Jesus Christ as your Lord and Savior? It is as simple as ABC.

A = Admit that your sins have separated you from a holy God. Romans 3:23 says that, "all have sinned and fallen short of the glory of God".

B = Believe that Jesus' death on the cross atoned for your sins and He rose from the dead to be our high priest before the Father in heaven. Someday He is coming back for those who love and serve Him, (See John 3:16).

C = Commit your life to Christ by turning from your sins (repentance), confessing your faith in Christ, and being buried with Christ in the watery grave of baptism.

Repentance is a lifelong process of giving Jesus control of our lives. Every day we must commit ourselves to follow Christ, (Acts 26:20).

Then, we must confess our faith in Christ, not just once, but throughout life. In this way, we not only reaffirm our faith, but honor Christ and propagate the Gospel, (Romans 10:9-10).

Finally, we must be baptized into Christ. This is a burial in water, depicting the death, burial, and resurrection of Christ, (Romans 6:3-5). Our scripture today promises that a penitent believer who is baptized into Christ receives the forgiveness of sins and gift of the Holy Spirit, (Acts 2:38).

PRAYER THOUGHTS - Lord, these steps to salvation are simple, but not always easy. May we obey them so we can spend eternity with You.

BEAR FRUIT OR DIE

SCRIPTURE READING - Luke 13:6-9

The immediate message of the parable of the barren fig tree is Israel's disobedience and God's patience. Israel is represented by the fig tree and God by the owner of the vineyard. Jesus is the vine dresser who came to give Israel, and all of us, a second chance. If we reject the Messiah, God's only alternative is judgment.

When it comes to this matter of bearing fruit for God, I have noticed that there are at least three kinds of people. First of all, bored are the barren. There is nothing more boring than living to please and pamper oneself. True meaning and fulfillment in life are found in serving God and others.

Secondly, burdened are the busy. The problem here is that activity can become an idol. We can become church workaholics and neglect our family and even our health.

Finally, blessed are the balanced. In our devotion to Christ, we ought to pray for wisdom to keep God, family, work, and recreation in their proper place and priority. We must not compartmentalize our lives. By that I mean we should not say, "This part of my life is for God, that part for family, the other for work, etc." No, each facet of our lives intersects and impacts the others and God must be over all.

PRAYER THOUGHTS - Merciful Father, we praise you for your long-suffering during our dry spells and going astray. Thank you for being a God of second chances. May we respond to your grace lest we come under your judgment.

WHO'S NUMBER ONE?

SCRIPTURE READING - Luke 14:15-24

As Christians we are called to support the Lord's work with our time and finances. The Bible is clear that God has a claim on our resources.

In today's scripture, Jesus told the parable of the great banquet. He has invited people to come to the great banquet and there are three excuses given. The first one said, "I have just bought a field and I must go and see it. Please excuse me." Another one said, "I have just bought five yoke of oxen and am on my way to try them out. Please excuse me." Still another said, "I just got married, so I can't come."

This parable illustrates things we may value more than God. The first example represents our possessions, the second is our work, and the third is our relationships.

The lesson is clear: We cannot give God what belongs to Him if He has to play second fiddle to other priorities. He is either Lord of all or He is not Lord at all.

You see, when it comes to your giving, it is not how much time, talent, or money you have. It is how much Christ you have. Until Jesus has first place in your life, you will have giving problems. When you put Him first, giving will become natural and joyful.

PRAYER THOUGHTS - Lord, all we have is on loan from You. How we use it is a test. Help us to pass that test.

HOW, THEN, SHALL WE GIVE?

SCRIPTURE READING - 2 Corinthians 9:6-11

One of my favorite comic strips is "The Wizard of Id". Some time ago the cartoon showed a knight and his wife, baby in arms, walking out of church. The wife says to the friar, "I apologize for my baby crying in church. She's teething."

The friar replied, "No problem. But why was your husband crying?"

She said, "He's tithing."

Sometimes meeting our obligations is painful, even when giving to the Lord. It is easy to think when we drop our offering into the plate, "I'll never see that money again." But Jesus says that is the only money we ever will see again because we are "laying up for ourselves treasures in heaven," (Matthew 6:19-20).

In our scripture today, Paul exhorts us to give cheerfully because we will reap generously if we sow generously. God will be no man's debtor. You cannot out-give God. Whatever you put into the Lord's hand will come back multiplied.

So, let's give God our best, knowing that He will return His best to us. And His best is far better than our best.

PRAYER THOUGHTS - Heavenly Father, please forgive our selfishness. The heavens and the earth belong to You. Help us to generously give back to You what is already Yours.

PASSIONATE FAITH

SCRIPTURE READING - 2 Peter 1:3-11

It has been said that there are three types of believers. There are those who know about God, those who actually know God, and a few who learn to enjoy God. To which group do you belong?

What are you doing to develop an appetite for a personal relationship with God? Today's scripture tells us that God is the source of all spiritual growth. We need His divine power to become more godly and Christ-like. But believers have personal responsibility to cultivate their own spiritual growth, while depending upon God's power. That is why Peter says, "Make every effort to add to your faith goodness," and so on. We must become passionate about our Christian development.

To be passionate spiritually means that we are enthusiastic about it. Biblical words for this might be "fervent" or "zealous". We are excited about our faith and it shows in our lifestyle and our witness to others.

Oswald Chambers said, "Human nature, if it is healthy, demands excitement. And if it does not find its excitement in the right way, it will seek it in the wrong way." Let us find our greatest joy in our personal relationship with God.

PRAYER THOUGHTS - Gracious Father, we are in awe of your desire to be at the very center of our lives. Create in us a passion to ever please and serve you.

THE POWER OF PRAYER

SCRIPTURE READING - Daniel 6:10-22

Daniel was a great man of God, and prayer was a factor in his spiritual power. He prayed regularly, morning, afternoon, and night. He confided in God and humbled himself before the Lord, (see his prayer in Daniel 9:1-19).

Daniel saw all of life from God's perspective, so prayer was a natural outgrowth of that relationship. As a child, you may have been taught that prayer was reserved for mealtimes, bedtime, and church services. Many carry this misconception into adulthood. But God wants to be in constant communication with us throughout every day. We should share with Him all of our experiences and feelings, just as we do with family members and close friends.

When we pray about everything, we open ourselves up to receive God's guidance and blessings. Let me give you an example. When I leave town sometimes, I am listening to the local radio station. The further from home I get, the weaker the signal becomes. When I turn around and head back home, the station comes in more clearly as I draw closer to town.

Our relationship with God works like that. When we draw close to Him in prayer, we hear His voice more clearly. That is why Jesus commanded his disciples, "Watch and pray so that you do not fall into temptation," (Matthew 26:41). The Lord's voice will call us to the way of love, joy, and peace. But we must listen to Him in prayer and through study of His Word.

PRAYER THOUGHTS - Heavenly Father, we need Your provision and protection every hour of every day. May our prayer lives reflect our dependence upon You.

CHURCH GROWTH

SCRIPTURE READING - Acts 2:41, 47; 6:7

The early church experienced rapid growth. Why is it that many churches today are plateaued or in decline? Most church leaders desire growth, but desire alone is not enough. We must be willing to prepare for growth.

How do we prepare? First of all, we must be aware of some statistics. The average church loses ten percent of its members each year. Two to three percent of their members move away, one to two percent die, and four to six percent are reversions (They drop out of church or switch churches). This means that if a church has annual additions amounting to ten percent of their average attendance, they are experiencing zero growth. They are merely replacing those who are leaving each year. In other words, for a church to have a net gain of ten percent annually, they need additions totaling twenty percent of their average attendance every year.

If a church grows by ten percent per year, it can double its attendance every 7.4 years. In order to do that, the members of the church must be willing to pay the price. The price is making every group in the church fifty percent non-members. It means having a lot of people with problems in their fellowship because unsaved people are outside of Christ and often have messed-up lives. It will require members to give more generously of their time, talents, and treasure because meeting the needs of hurting people is costly. Many churches don't grow because they won't pay the price.

PRAYER THOUGHTS - Heavenly Father, stir up our love for lost souls. Make us willing to expend the necessary effort and resources in order to see lives changed by Jesus Christ.

SHOW AND TELL

SCRIPTURE READING - Matthew 25:31-46

The world is not going to be impressed by the message Christians tell unless they see us showing a Jesus kind of love to others. We must do good deeds while we share the good news if we expect to reach the lost.

Jesus is our example here. Can you imagine Jesus going out into towns and villages during his public ministry and proclaiming his gospel without accompanying acts of healing and helping? Do we really think our Savior would have gained a hearing (much less a following) or established the credibility of his message without displaying some proof that his gospel was real?

In the Sermon on the Mount, when Jesus talks about his followers being the light of the world, he concludes by saying, "...Let your light shine before men, that they may see your good deeds and praise your Father in heaven," (Matthew 5:16).

What does Jesus mean here by "good deeds"? It certainly refers to religious deeds we do because we are Christians (worship, evangelism, fellowship, etc.). It also includes holy deeds of purity, fidelity, and integrity. But we must not omit deeds of love, mercy, and justice extended to all people. When we show compassion and give aid to those outside the church, we greatly improve the odds that some of them will end up inside the church.

PRAYER THOUGHTS - Loving Father, empower us to be like Jesus and go about doing good so that doors may be opened for the Gospel.

COUNTING THE COST

SCRIPTURE READING - Luke 14:25-33

In his book, The Cost of Discipleship, Dietrich Bonhoeffer says, "Those who believe, obey, and only those who obey, truly believe." That is basically what Jesus is saying in today's scripture. If we say, "yes" to Jesus, it means saying, "no" to many other persons or things.

While such a commitment is costly, it is still the best bargain in the universe. Why? Because Jesus has much more to offer us than we can ever give to him. However, if we do not give Jesus everything we have, we cannot receive everything he has to bestow upon us. To the extent that we surrender to him, to that extent he can bless us.

When Jesus says we must "hate" even our family members in order to be his disciples, he is using hyperbole. That is, an exaggerated comparison not to be taken literally. He is saying that our love for him must become strong enough that no other person can come between him and us. Jesus must come first to a disciple even if it requires renouncing all other allegiances.

Some may mistakenly conclude here that loving Jesus more means loving your family less. Not so. When you give the Lord one hundred percent of what you have, you are a greater blessing to your family. You have divine power to love others more deeply and righteously.

So, giving it all to Jesus is not ultimately giving up anything that is worthwhile and enduring. It is accessing everything that really matters.

PRAYER THOUGHTS - Father, you opened up the treasure house of heaven when you gave us Jesus. Help us to totally surrender to him that we may tap more deeply into those blessings.

KNOWING GOD

SCRIPTURE READING - Psalm 100

C. S. Lewis said, "The man who has God and everything has no more than the man who has God alone."

I Timothy 6:6 says, "…Godliness with contentment is great gain." In other words, if you are a godly person and are content with what you have, you are rich. Period!

One of the most beautiful passages in the Bible is found in the ninth chapter of Jeremiah. It says, "This is what the Lord says: 'Let not the wise man boast of his wisdom or the strong man boast of his strength or the rich man boast of his riches, but let him who boasts boast about this: that he understands and knows me, that I am the Lord, who exercises kindness, justice and righteousness on earth, for in these I delight,' declares the Lord," (Jeremiah 9:23-24).

Can you boast of an intimate, vibrant, life-changing relationship with the Living God? I hope so, because in the end nothing else matters.

The famous American author, Mark Twain, and his daughter once toured Europe together. During their travels they were wined and dined by other famous literary giants, entertainers, business tycoons, kings, queens, and other celebrities. At one point during their trip, Twain's daughter said to him, "Dad, you know everybody but God, don't you?"

May that never be said of us.

PRAYER THOUGHTS - Heavenly Father, we bow before You as our Creator and the Giver of every good and perfect gift. May we never forget that our highest ambition should be to know and walk with You.

WHY WORSHIP FIZZLES

SCRIPTURE READING - I Corinthians 13

Love is the key that opens the door to deeper worship, fellowship and Christian service. Most people who are chronically disappointed with church services in reality have a heart problem.

For example, you could hire for your church the best worship leader on earth and he or she could revive your worship for a time. But if the hearts of your people do not change, within six months you will be right back where you started.

The fact is that if you are growing deeper in your love for God Monday through Saturday, then your worship on Sunday will be a spontaneous over-flow of your enthusiasm for the Lord. And if you are praying for and concerned about and loving your brothers and sisters in Christ Monday through Saturday, then your fellowship with them on Sunday will be what it ought to be.

Putting it bluntly, people who do not enjoy church are probably not Christians. You may not choose to go to church the same place I do, but if you love Jesus and love his people, you will want to worship somewhere. Love is so important that the Bible says it is a test whereby we can tell whether or not we are saved. I John 3:14 says, "We know that we have passed from death to life, because we love each other. Anyone who does not love remains in death."

PRAYER THOUGHTS - Lord, may we love you and others as you have loved us. And help our worship to be a sacrifice of praise for all you have done for us.

REAL LOVE PASSES THE TEST

SCRIPTURE READING - I John 4:7-12

One Sunday morning early in June, a church member shook my hand at the door and said, "Brian, I'm so glad you're here. I haven't heard one bad thing about you."

I smiled and said, "You will."

I wasn't trying to be a smart aleck, I just realize that in all human relationships you have the honeymoon phase. During that initial get-acquainted stage everybody puts their best foot forward but this is followed by the disillusionment phase. That is when the masks come off and we see that the other person has some defects after all.

It is easy to be sweet during the honeymoon. But our Christianity is tested when disillusionment sets in. When others get in our way is when our Christian love ought to shine its brightest. That is when we ought to remember Ephesians 4:32, "Be kind to each other, tender-hearted, forgiving each other, just as God in Christ has forgiven you."

On the other hand, if I am out of line, tell me. I am obligated to do the same for you (Leviticus 19:17; Galatians 6:1). Sometimes I think we are too "nice" in the church. We avoid confronting each other because we are afraid of being judgmental. Yet, most of the Bible consists of exhortations to those who needed correction.

Honeymoons are nice, but they are also a bit unreal. Let's be real with each other. That will help us to grow as individuals and as a church.

PRAYER THOUGHTS - Father, help us to remember that the test of our love is not how we treat those who like us, but how we behave toward those who mistreat us.

WHY WE NEED THE CHURCH

SCRIPTURE READING - Acts 2:42-47

The church of today may not be a clone of the early church with its communal living and continual miracles. But God intended that the fellowship of His people should be a source of blessing to each other and a powerful witness to the world.

Sometimes we encounter those who say something like, "Give me Jesus, but you can keep the church." Often they have been disappointed or even hurt by those who are brothers or sisters in Christ. This is unfortunate, but not unusual. The church is a family and families have conflicts. Christians are redeemed, but not yet perfected.

As Christians, we have Jesus as our Savior, God as our Father, and the church is to be our mother. I think this latter idea has in many cases been lost. The church is treated more today like a business. True, the church has a little business side to it, but the primary work of the church is that of mother. Cyprian, in the early church, said, "He who hath not the church for his mother, hath not God for his father."

The church is mother because it nourishes, nurtures, disciplines, and brings us from immaturity to maturity. None of us had a perfect mother and you will never find a perfect church. But we still need both of these in our lives.

PRAYER THOUGHTS - Heavenly Father, we praise you for your great salvation and for your wisdom in putting us into a spiritual earthly family. May we always love the fellowship of believers and allow ourselves to be loved by them.

DECIDING NOT TO DECIDE

SCRIPTURE READING - Acts 2:42

Walter Miller of Stone Mountain, Georgia, wrote: "Concerning ambivalence, I have mixed feelings." Mixed feelings are a normal part of life. Sort of like the young man I heard about who was visiting with his girlfriend's father. Her dad said, "So, you want to be my son-in-law?"

He replied, "Not really, but if I marry your daughter, I don't see how I can avoid it."

Many situations in life cause us to be ambivalent, torn between two emotions. But when it comes to spiritual matters, God's children should be marked by faith and conviction.

One time a Christian lady shared this experience with my wife. She said, "For a long time I would get up on Tuesday mornings and ask myself, 'Well, am I going to Ladies' Bible study today or not?' Then one Tuesday I got up and said, 'I'm not going to ask myself that question anymore. I'm just going to be in Bible study every Tuesday.'"

This was one wise lady. Decide now not to decide week by week whether or not you will go to church. Make a commitment to worship with your Christian brothers and sisters regularly. Do not get caught in the trap of asking yourself each Sunday, "Well, am I going to church today or not?" Do what you know will please the Lord and encourage other believers, (Hebrews 10:25).

PRAYER THOUGHTS - Lord, forgive us for those times we have allowed trivial pursuits to keep us away from your house. We resolve to make fellowship with your people the priority it needs to be.

CARING ENOUGH TO CONFRONT

SCRIPTURE READING - Galatians 6:1-5

Today's scripture is clear about the attitude and action a Christian should take when observing another believer who is caught in a sin. Our attitude should be loving, humble, and concerned. The action we should take is to approach the wrongdoer gently and urge him or her to do the right thing.

Unfortunately, we often tend to do the opposite of what God requires. Most Christians seldom call upon anybody to repent of a sin and make necessary changes. At the same time, we may sit back and judge an erring saint with a critical and self-righteous spirit.

The Bible calls us to turn this scenario completely around. We must care enough to confront those who are straying, but need to check our own attitude before we do so. Ephesians 4:25 commands us to speak the truth to one another. It is better to speak the truth, even though it hurts at first, because the truth has the potential to heal in the long run. And, telling the truth is more likely to bring healing if we "speak the truth in love," (Ephesians 4:15). While doing all this, remember Paul's warning, "But watch yourself, or you also may be tempted," (Galatians 6:1b).

PRAYER THOUGHTS - Lord, give us your heart of compassion for those who have wandered from Your will. Guide us as we seek to call them back to You.

A PEP TALK

SCRIPTURE READING - Joshua 1:1-9

Did it really happen? A sailor walked into a U. S. Navy recruiting office. He asked to speak to the man who recruited him. When the recruiter walked into the room, the dejected sailor said, "Would you give me the same sales pitch you gave me two years ago? I need it."

Many do not reenlist in the armed forces because the realities of military life often fall short of their expectations. Likewise, the rigors of serving in the Lord's army have discouraged many formerly stalwart warriors.

When this happens to me, I like to LOOK BACK, LOOK IN, and LOOK UP. I look back and remember that God has never let me down in the past and He will not forsake me now. Then I look in and make sure that I am motivated by love for God and love for others. When I forget to do that is when I start feeling sorry for myself.

Finally, I need to look up. Usually when I get discouraged, it is because I am focusing more on the problems before me than on the power behind me. The Lord gives me exactly what I need to do what He has called me to do. I need to think vertically, not horizontally. Then I have the courage to move ahead with the assignment He has given me.

If I am still discouraged after taking those steps, I am probably just tired and need some rest or I am trying to do something God never intended for me to do.

PRAYER THOUGHTS - Almighty God, we know that You have not brought us this far only to let us down. Help us to remember that You will empower us to do what You have called us to do.

CHRIST IN PROPHECY

SCRIPTURE READING - Isaiah 53:3-6

Jesus Christ is the central figure of the largest religion on earth. Christianity is the only religion foretold in prophecy. In fact, no other person was described in prophecy other than John the Baptist, but not even he in such vast detail. The Old Testament, written centuries before the birth of Christ, contains more than three hundred prophecies concerning his coming.

For example, Isaiah 52:13-53:12 contains a dozen predictions about the life and work of Christ. Genesis 49:10 and Jeremiah 23:5-6 tell us about his ancestral lineage.

Isaiah 7:14 predicts that he will be born of a virgin. Micah 5:2 prophesies that he will be born in Bethlehem. The time of Messiah's appearing is foretold in Daniel 9:24-27. Psalm 118:22 says he will be rejected by his people. The miracles of Jesus were foretold in Isaiah 35:4-6. His resurrection was predicted in Psalm 16:10. Details about his crucifixion are given in Exodus 12:46, Psalm 22:16-18, and Zechariah 12:10. Isaiah 9:6-7 tells us that Jesus will be God in human flesh and will establish an everlasting Kingdom.

We could go on, but you get the idea. Our faith in Jesus is verified by supernatural predictive insight. That is one reason why Christians confidently worship Jesus Christ as the King of Kings and Savior of the world!

PRAYER THOUGHTS - Sovereign Lord, we believe in you because you fulfilled all that the prophets wrote about you in ancient times. Please empower us as we prepare ourselves and others for your soon return.

FORGIVENESS AND RECONCILIATION

SCRIPTURE READING - Matthew 18:21-35

The parable of the unforgiving servant in our scripture reading presents a simple yet profound lesson. Our Holy God has been sinned against over and over by each of us. He has suffered loss and paid the debt that we might be forgiven. He asks us to extend the same mercy and grace to others. Failure to do so invites God's judgment, (See Matthew 6:14-15; James 2:13).

This is difficult because forgiveness is something that must be given before it is felt. You refuse to treat like an enemy the person who hurt you even though they treated you like an enemy. You pray for them and attempt to build a bridge to them. You refrain from slandering their name or wishing them to suffer for their meanness. As a result, you become more Christ-like and experience peace rather than bitterness.

The bottom line is that Christians are never to give up on each other, never to give up on a relationship, and never to write-off another believer. We must never tire of forgiving (and repenting!) and seeking to repair our relationships. Matthew 5:23-24 tells us we should go to someone if we have offended them. Matthew 18:15-17 says we should go to someone if they have offended us. In other words, whether we sin against another or they sin against us, it is always our responsibility to make the first move. That is how important forgiveness and reconciliation are to God!

PRAYER THOUGHTS - Father, we confess that you have cancelled our great debt of sin. Give us grace to do the same for those who have wronged us.

EXPERIENCING CHRISTIAN FELLOWSHIP

SCRIPTURE READING - Acts 2:42-47

What is fellowship? Why is it important? How do we get it?

The word "fellowship" carries the idea of sharing our lives with one another. This was exemplified in the life of the early church. Acts 2:44 says, "All the believers were together and had everything in common." The Lord calls all His followers into the spiritual family of the church.

We experience fellowship by voluntarily entering into four relationships with God's people. The first relationship is membership. We choose to belong to a church family. Then we choose friendship, which involves learning to share with others. After belonging to a local church for a while, we ought to enter into partnership with it, which means doing our part by involvement in some kind of ministry responsibilities. Finally comes kinship, when you learn to love believers like family.

I Peter 2:17 says that we are to "love the family of believers". We need to be needed and we also need the encouragement of Christian brothers and sisters. These are people with whom we will spend eternity. Christian friends are friends forever. We do spiritual battle together against the "forces of darkness" in an unbelieving world. Through our united witness, more people can be won to Christ than we could ever win by working alone. That is why the church is called "the body of Christ," (I Corinthians 12:27).

Christ is the head and we are His body on earth. Let us join it, enjoy it, and build it up!

PRAYER THOUGHTS - Lord, we thank You that in Your wisdom You have placed us in a spiritual family where we can serve and be served. May Your love flow through us to our Christian brothers and sisters.

DO I HAVE TO GO TO CHURCH?

SCRIPTURE READING - Hebrews 10:19-25

Asking the question, "Do I have to go to church?" is a lot like asking, "Do I have to kiss my spouse?" Neither question is asked by someone who loves. People who do not love the church, however, will probably never ask that question. They simply will not show up at church very often.

The Bible says that the church is the body of Christ, (I Corinthians 12:27). Jesus is the head of the church. So if we separate ourselves from the body of Christ, we are also disconnected from the head. That is a dangerous place to be.

In I Peter 2:17, we are commanded to "love the brotherhood of believers". The church is our spiritual family on earth. As Christians, we have family privileges and obligations. We need the church and the church needs us. Out in the world, believers are in the minority. This can wear us down if we do not gather regularly with other people of faith.

One day a man said to me, "I can worship God just as well in my fishing boat as I can in church."

I replied, "That may be true, but if the fish get to biting, you might lose your sense of the Almighty."

However, we do not dictate to God how we will worship Him. He has told us how He wants to be worshiped in prescribed ritual. Besides that, worship is not the only reason for going to church. We may also go there for education, fellowship, ministry, and even evangelism.

PRAYER THOUGHTS - Lord, we thank you for giving us brothers and sisters who also love and serve you. Strengthen us to be a blessing to and with our spiritual family, the church.

HAPPINESS VS FULFILLMENT

SCRIPTURE READING - Matthew 16:24-27

No object or person other than God is worthy of our worship. For that reason, He also deserves our obedience.

The biggest competition God has for our allegiance is our own desires. As fallen creatures we tend to put our own wants first, then rationalize that we are doing God's will. For example, many people have said to me, "What I am doing is making me miserable and I know this can't be God's will because He wants me to be happy."

You will have a difficult time finding any scripture for that. As a matter of fact, God has not called us to be happy. He has called us to be obedient to His commands. When we are obedient, He will see that ultimately we are fulfilled and our lives have meaning.

In today's scripture, Jesus calls us to self-denial and sacrifice if we would be His followers. In another place Jesus told His disciples, "In this world you will have trouble. But take heart! I have overcome the world," (John 16:33b).

In Christ we enjoy peace of mind in life and in death. Our self-esteem is healthy because of the value God places on us and by the fellowship of the Holy Spirit who is always with us, (2 Corinthians 13:14). The devil only comes to steal and kill and destroy, Jesus comes "that we may have life, and have it to the full," (John 10:10).

PRAYER THOUGHTS - Lord, give us faith to pay the price of seeking first Your Kingdom. Help us to remember that the fruit of such sacrifice is always worth whatever it costs.

KEEP YOUR SALTINESS

SCRIPTURE READING - Matthew 5:13; Colossians 4:5-6

When Jesus tells His followers to keep their "saltiness," He means that we are to make the Gospel tasty. We are in the people business. The Bible calls us "ambassadors for Christ," (2 Corinthians 5:20). The Lord's honor is at stake in how we conduct ourselves. If people think of us as arrogant or mean or manipulative, they will avoid us. We will have no testimony for Jesus with those people.

Someone says, "I don't care what people think," but Jesus did. That's why He warned us about losing our saltiness. Salt seasons, it penetrates, it purifies, and it preserves. That is how we ought to influence our culture.

The Pharisees accused Jesus of eating with sinners. Of course He did. He wanted them to know that He was their friend. The Pharisees were too proud to eat with sinners.

We must also protect each other's saltiness if we want to have influence for Christ in the community. If we are openly critical of the church, her leaders, and members, we will have little impact for Christ where we live.

Somebody says, "Isn't it important for us to live a godly life?" Of course it is. Another asks, "Don't you believe Bible knowledge is crucial?" Absolutely, doctrine and morals are important, but don't lose your saltiness.

PRAYER THOUGHTS - Lord, give us wisdom to earn the respect of others that we may influence them for You.

YOU CAN LIVE A HOLY LIFE

SCRIPTURE READING - I John 1:5-2:1

In our scripture for today, the Apostle John exhorts his Christian readers not to sin. Then he tells them what to do if they do sin. John is not being spiritually schizophrenic. Believers will slip up and fall short at times. They will "miss the mark," which is the primary meaning of the Greek word "hamartia," which is translated "sin".

However, Christians must not sin deliberately or intentionally, (see Hebrews 10:26). Our text says that if we have fellowship with God, we will not "walk in the darkness". True believers practice a lifestyle of obedience to God and His Word.

The blood of Christ not only saves us from the guilt of sin, but also the power of sin in our lives. We no longer have to serve sin. The Holy Spirit gives us the power to serve Christ, (see Galatians 5:16).

Many Christians seldom experience the victory over sin they desire. They are trying to fight the devil in the strength of the flesh, and overlook the great reservoir of power available to them through the Holy Spirit.

"For we know that our old self was crucified with him so that the body of sin might be done away with, that we should no longer be slaves to sin…" (Romans 6:6).

PRAYER THOUGHTS - Heavenly Father, we desire above all else to please you in everything we do. Help us to enter into the victory over sin that has already been won for us by the Lord Jesus.

PAUL'S PRAYER ADVICE

SCRIPTURE READING - Colossians 4:2-4

Verse two of today's scripture says, "Devote yourselves to prayer, being watchful and thankful." God's Word says that we are to be devoted to prayer. We understand what it means to be devoted. We talk about a lady who is a devoted mother. She makes her children a high priority. Do we make prayer a high priority in our daily lives? When we have a busy day, is prayer the last thing we give up or is it the first?

Not only does Colossians 4:2 exhort us to be devoted to prayer, we are also told to be watchful. We are to expect God to act in response to our petitions. We should also be aware that the Lord may prompt us to take action which will help fulfill our requests for divine assistance. Finally, our watchfulness applies to spiritual warfare. Watch out for Satan's attempts to deceive and distract.

As we watch Gods power unleashed in response to prayer, we will have cause to "be thankful". Over and over again the Scriptures command that we accompany our requests to God with thanksgiving. It seems that God's ears are more open to those who appreciate what He has already done. When we pray, we should expect heavenly provision. Otherwise, we are choosing to be satisfied merely with what is humanly possible.

PRAYER THOUGHTS - Almighty God, we thank You for being a prayer-hearing and prayer-answering God. Forgive us when we neglect prayer and dilute Your power in our lives.

THE CHURCH ON PURPOSE

SCRIPTURE READING - Ephesians 4:11-16

What is the purpose of the church? The New Testament emphasizes two primary tasks: to evangelize the lost and edify the saved. These two priorities have one overarching purpose, as illustrated in the following conversation.

A seminary professor told of a student who asked him, "So, the purpose of the church is to grow, right?"

The professor rightly replied, "No, the purpose of the church is to glorify God."

The Apostle Paul would agree with this professor. In Romans 15:6, he wrote that when the church does what it was designed to do, we will "glorify the God and Father of our Lord Jesus Christ".

Our scripture for today tells us that when members of the church function properly, "the body of Christ" will be "built up". The emphasis here is on spiritual growth that God's people may "become mature, attaining to the whole measure of the fullness of Christ".

This brings us back to the purpose of the church. How does the church make decisions about what needs to be done? Some churches are driven by tradition. They are committed to preserving the status quo. Others are driven by finances. They will only do it if the money is on hand. Still other churches are driven by strong personalities. If the right person wants it done, it will happen. But the churches God blesses the most are those who prayerfully seek to do His will for His glory.

PRAYER THOUGHTS - Lord, we thank you for the Body of Christ on earth. Help those of us who belong to it to work together in harmony and unity to the praise of Your glory.

ARE YOU MARRIED TO A "10"?

SCRIPTURE READING - Proverbs 31:10-31

A CBS News survey showed that sixty percent of Americans see themselves as being above average in looks (an 8-10 on a scale of 1-10). This is obviously unrealistic, but it shows how human nature flatters itself.

This news story reminded me of an incident when I got myself into a little bit of trouble over this very subject. My wife and I were visiting our daughter and son-in-law. We somehow started talking about rating the looks of family members on a scale of 1-10. It started with rating our grandchildren, but ended up with rating each other. My son-in-law said to me, "I am surprised that you didn't rate your wife and daughter as 10's."

Then they both looked at me as if to say, "What don't you like about us?"

Nothing I said could dig me out of the hole I was in.

After reflecting on this scenario for a while, here is what I came up with. Rating each other 1-10 on looks seems like a rather superficial way of judging someone. Then I recalled being with a group of bachelors in seminary many years ago and talking about choosing a wife. We came up with the five S's: Spiritual, Sweet, Smart, Strong and Sexy. I give my wife a "10" in all five categories. That is a very different thing than saying she does or does not look like a movie star. Being a physical "10" is not the most important thing in choosing a spouse. Even being "sexy" (romantically attractive) involves much more than mere physical beauty. Far more important are spiritual compatibility, delighting in each other's, company and sharing core values. Wouldn't you agree?

PRAYER THOUGHTS - Lord, there is only so much we can do to make and keep ourselves physically attractive. Help us to remember that we can have as much of your Spirit as we are willing to receive. May that inner beauty grow in us so that we will honor You.

CORRECTION VS CONDEMNATION

SCRIPTURE READING - Matthew 7:1-5

A preacher had on his desk a special book labeled: "Complaints of Members Against One Another". When one of his people came to tell him the faults of another, he would say, "Well, here's my complaint book. I'll write down what you say and you can sign it. Then when I have to take up the matter officially, I will know what I can expect you to testify to."

The sight of the open book and ready pen had its effect.

"Oh no, I couldn't sign anything like that," and no entry was made. The preacher said he kept the book for thirty years, opened it hundreds of times, and never wrote a line in it.

The Bible is clear that when we see someone going astray, we should go to them ourselves, (Galatians 6:1; James 5:20). We should go to lovingly encourage, not self-righteously condemn.

At other times, we may be on the receiving end of criticism. If that happens, don't get paranoid, lose your temper, go into a "shell," or attack the other person. Prayerfully consider suggestions from constructive critics. But keep cool and ignore nit-pickers. Seek to please God, and God's people will usually be pleased with you.

PRAYER THOUGHTS - Father, help us to care enough to confront those who are wandering from the straight and narrow. At the same time, give us the humility to accept correction when we need it ourselves.

QUIET TIME

SCRIPTURE READING - Luke 10:38-42

Solitude with God is not an easy thing for most of us to schedule. Yet, it is something we must make time for and jealously guard. Jesus did it and so must we. Without intense times alone with God, we soon lose our identity as His children. We will allow others to shape our hearts and actions more than He does.

Our primary purpose as Christians is not to focus on learning, on people, or even on our ministries. Our ultimate objective is to walk with God, (see I John 1:5-7). In our scripture for today, Jesus was teaching Martha that physical food can wait, but spiritual food cannot be neglected. We need to feed on God's Word and commune with Him through prayer. In order to do this, we must regularly make time to shut out all distractions so we can talk to and listen to Him.

One thing we notice in the life of Jesus is that the more intense the demands of his ministry became, the more time he took to be alone with the Father. This solitude is not privacy, which we Americans seem to consider a God-given right. Nor is it isolation, but rather we are talking about Presence with a capital "P". We need frequent periods of maximum-intensity intimacy with God if we expect to become more like Him.

PRAYER THOUGHTS - Heavenly Father, teach us how to be still and to know that You are God. Help us to walk with You, not only in those quiet moments, but always.

CHERISHING GOD'S PROMISES

SCRIPTURE READING - Psalm 37:1-7

Nothing is more precious to me than the promises of God. Recently, I made a list of my favorite promises from God's Word. Here they are:

Acts 2:38 - This is the first New Covenant command with a promise attached to it. It is actually two commandments and two promises.

I John 1:9 - After baptism, forgiveness of sins is available for the asking.

I Corinthians 10:13 - Christians need never be overpowered by temptation.

Philippians 4:6-7 - Prayer makes possible the peace that surpasses all understanding.

James 1:5-7 - God will give us all the wisdom we need if we ask for it in faith.

Matthew 28:18-20 - Promise of the Lord's presence

2 Chronicles 16:9a - Promise of God's strength

Philippians 4:19 - Promise of God's provision

Psalm 91 - Promise of God's protection

Romans 8:28 - Those who love and follow the Lord are assured that no matter what happens to them, all things will work together for good. Why not come up with your own list of favorite promises and then commit them to memory?

PRAYER THOUGHTS - Heavenly Father, may we never take Your promises for granted, but may we rather be strengthened by claiming them.

ENDURING PERSECUTION

SCRIPTURE READING - Matthew 5:1-12

Jesus gives a blessing to those who are persecuted for righteousness' sake. They are like the prophets and their reward in heaven will be great.

Sometimes we get to thinking that something is wrong with the church if the world hates us. But the New Testament is clear that followers of Christ will be despised and rejected by the world. Jesus said that the world hates him because he condemns their evil deeds, (John 7:7). Christ also warned that the world would persecute his followers, (John 15:20). Jesus said in Matthew 10:22, "You will be hated by everyone because of me, but the one who stands firm to the end will be saved."

Persecution may take many forms such as slander, being ostracized, fired from work, being imprisoned, tortured, or even put to death. The Lord, in his letter to the church in Smyrna (Revelation 2:10), said, "Be faithful, even to the point of death, and you will receive the crown of life," (see also Hebrews 11:32-40).

On the other hand, Revelation 21:8 tells us that the "cowardly" will not make it to heaven. The word used here does not refer to common fears such as being afraid of water or spiders or high places. Rather, it refers to persecution when we must choose between standing up for Jesus or denying faith in Him. May God give us courage to take our stand whatever the cost.

PRAYER THOUGHTS - Lion of Judah, empower us to fight the good fight of faith, even when we must endure strong opposition. May we claim your promises to those who suffer for the Gospel.

PREACH THE WORD

SCRIPTURE READING - Romans 10:8-15

Paul stresses the importance of preaching or proclaiming God's Word so that people may be saved. Jesus commanded in the Great Commission that we go everywhere to tell others the good news of salvation, (Matthew 28:18-20; Mark 16:15-16).

After we come into Christ, we still need preaching and teaching to help us grow in our faith and to keep us on the "straight and narrow". Again, the Great Commission says we are to "teach them to obey everything I have commanded you."

Being a preacher is similar to being a dietician for a school, hospital, etc. You want what you serve to be both nutritional and tasty. Your goal is to have a balance that will meet the needs of those entrusted to your care. Some messages, like some meals, are tastier than others. For example, people would rather hear about God's forgiveness than to be told they need to repent of their sins. However, both messages are needed for a balanced biblical diet.

Whether we are sharing the Gospel with those outside of Christ or proclaiming God's Word to veteran believers, we must leave the results to God. Paul wrote, "I planted the seed, Apollos watered it, but God made it grow," (I Corinthians 3:6). May we be found faithful in sharing the Word of Life!

PRAYER THOUGHTS - God of hope, You have given us the greatest message in all the earth. Help us to use every means at our disposal to get Your Word out to all people both near and far.

SALT AND LIGHT

SCRIPTURE READING - Matthew 5:13-16

When our American forefathers signed the Declaration of Independence, Benjamin Franklin said to the other signers, "Now we must hang together, or they shall surely hang us separately." They knew that in choosing to revolt against Mother England they could be signing their own death warrants.

A similar thing happens when we elect to revolt against this world's system and take our stand with Jesus Christ. We become aliens and strangers to most of those around us. "The world," a biblical term for unbelievers, hates us for following Jesus Christ because they hate him, (see Matthew 10:22).

Jesus has called us to be "salt" and "light". Salt purifies and preserves. It also bites and stings. Light exposes the darkness. The attitude that evil will triumph is demonic. Believers are called to be the moral conscience of the community. We must give push-back to the world. All that is necessary for evil to triumph is for good people to do nothing.

PRAYER THOUGHTS - Righteous Father, give us holy boldness to be witnesses for Christ and to uphold godly values to the world around us.

LIVING ABUNDANTLY

SCRIPTURE READING - John 10:1-10

In today's scripture, Jesus warns us against trading eternal joy for temporary pleasure. The devil offers us many things that look quite attractive on the surface, but the Evil One only comes "to steal and kill and destroy". Many things which appear worth living for are temporary substitutes for the riches God wants to give us.

Unbelievers make gods out of pursuing riches, knowledge, success, power, popularity, physical fitness, and sensual thrills (sex, food, etc.). They may also make a god out of "making a positive difference" in the world. Many good causes are not worthy of our ultimate allegiance because they perish with the end of this life or this world.

In John 10:10 Jesus promises his disciples a full and abundant life. The Lord does not merely give us the bare essentials of life, but he promises us a life that is meaningful, fulfilling, and everlasting. In this life we have joy, peace, and the fellowship of the Holy Spirit, plus the best of everything in the eternal age to come. In this world we will have trouble, but Jesus has overcome the world, (See John 16:33).

The gods of planet earth cannot satisfy, but you can be satisfied in Christ. "Blessed are those who hunger and thirst for righteousness, for they shall be satisfied," (Matthew 5:6).

PRAYER THOUGHTS - Heavenly Father, we praise you for calling us out of the darkness of this world and into your marvelous light. May we ever experience and share the abundant life that is found only in Christ.

NOT ALL SIN IS EQUAL

SCRIPTURE READING - Hebrews 10:26-31

People often minimize their sinful behavior by saying something like, "Yes, what I'm doing is wrong, but we are all sinners." This is true. However, the Bible teaches that there are two types of sin. The first type of sin occurs even in devoted believers and qualifies for God's pardon. The second type of sin reveals a heart of unbelief and receives God's condemnation.

I John 1:8 says that if we claim to be without sin we are deceiving ourselves. This refers to type one sin. It means to "miss the mark". It was used of archers who try to hit the bullseye of a target with their arrow, but often miss. This relates to those sins when we want to do God's will but frequently fail.

The second type of sin is referred to in our scripture reading, (v. 26). It is premeditated, deliberate, and defiant sin. I John 1:6 speaks of those who "walk in darkness". They are in effect saying, "God, I know this is wrong, but I intend to do it anyway." If we go that direction and do not repent, we will face God's fiery judgment, (see again Hebrews 10:26-27).

PRAYER THOUGHTS - Lord of compassion, we thank you for your grace and forgiveness when we fall short of your glory. Keep us from having rebellious hearts which turn aside from the path of righteousness.

HOW DO YOU SERVE?

SCRIPTURE READING - Romans 12:6-8

The great musician and composer Ludwig Beethoven was once approached by a young man, age twenty, who asked him, "How can I learn to compose great symphonies like you do?"

Beethoven replied, "Start by writing simple tunes and work your way up."

The young man said, "But you were writing symphonies when you were seven years old."

"Yes," answered Beethoven, "but nobody had to tell me how to do it."

What is it that God has made it easy for you to do? One thing I have enjoyed doing since childhood is writing. When I was ten years old, I edited my own little newspaper. When I was eleven, I won an essay contest. As a high school student, I wrote my first article to be published in a national magazine.

I enjoy the challenge of writing these brief devotional thoughts. It is fun for me to take a big subject and try to boil it down to 300 words or less. While I enjoy writing, I know some people who find that task to be pure torture.

All of us should discover our gifts. What is it that makes time fly for you? That is probably an area where you have talent. God gives us these gifts to serve others, not to make us proud. The Bible says, "For what makes you different from anyone else? What do you have that you did not receive? And if you did receive it, why do you boast as though you did not?" (I Corinthians 4:7).

So, what do you enjoy doing that you can use in service to God? Dedicate that skill to honor the Lord and He will bless you for it.

PRAYER THOUGHTS - Sovereign Lord, thank you for giving to us so that we may give back to you and others. Enable us to be humble servants for your glory.

DON'T BE LUKEWARM

SCRIPTURE READING - Revelation 3:14-22

In our scripture today, Jesus tells the church in Laodicea that He wishes they were either hot or cold; but since they are lukewarm, He will spit them out of His mouth. I used to think "hot" in that passage meant spiritually on fire, while "cold" indicated spiritual deadness. My misconception was a result of not understanding the geographical location of Laodicea.

The city of Laodicea is located in a valley between two other cities, Heiropolis and Colosse. Heiropolis was famous for its hot mineral springs where sick people went to bathe and find relief. Colosse was at the base of a mountain range and was blessed by many streams of pure, cold mountain water.

By the time the water flowed from Colosse down to Laodicea in the valley, it was no longer cold and by the time the water of Hieropolis reached Laodicea, it was not hot. The minerals of Heiropolis made the mountain water of Colosse taste like rotten eggs. The water in Laodicea was lukewarm and tasted terrible.

So, what was Jesus' lesson? He was saying, "I want you to be a person who invigorates others, like the cool, refreshing waters of Colosse or you can be a person who soothes those who are hurting, like the hot mineral waters of Hieropolis." Don't be lukewarm, 'out of the loop,' and worthless.

PRAYER THOUGHTS - Lord, help us to allow your love to flow through us that we might be a blessing to others.

BIBLE READING PLAN

SCRIPTURE READING - Acts 17:10-12

Most Christians realize that they ought to spend more time in the Scriptures. There are a number of reading plans which enable you to read through the Bible in one year. I have tried several of those over the years. Unfortunately, I have dropped out of most of them after a few weeks. My problem is that I get behind in the schedule and, realizing I'll never catch up, I just quit.

I do, however, have one Bible reading plan I have followed for almost sixty years. When I was ten years old, my grandmother gave me a Bible and encouraged me to read at least one chapter a day. I have done that pretty consistently all my life. Did you know that if you read just one chapter per day, you can read the entire Bible in two and a half years? That may sound like a snail's pace to you, but look at it this way: If you follow this plan for ten years, you will have read through the Bible four times. How many Christians have read every book of the Bible four times? Not very many.

As I read, I flip-flop back and forth between the Old and New Testaments so I don't get bogged down. As our scripture for today points out, it is not enough to listen to the Word being preached or to hear it being taught. We must study it for ourselves in a personal and regular way. If you are not doing this, now would be a good time to start.

PRAYER THOUGHTS - Lord, Your Word is "the bread of life" for our souls. Help us to find a way to feed on it every day.

COME CLEAN WITH GOD

SCRIPTURE READING - I John 1:5-10

It's spring and many of us feel like getting a fresh start this time of year. I think that is one of the motivations for spring cleaning. We have been cooped up all winter and we want to clear out the clutter and freshen up the house for the warmer months to come.

Spring is also a good time of year for spiritual house cleaning. We need to come clean with God and clear out the sinful clutter that fogs up our Christian lives. A good place to begin this process is to confess our sins to God.

Sometimes it is difficult to confess sin because we rationalize it. If we fail to recognize the presence of sin, we will become defensive and will not confess it to God. Sin distorts our thinking. When people become involved in sin, they lose common sense. Have you ever noticed that? They just lose all sense of reason. And you will hear people say things like, "Well, I think pornography enhances our relationship," or "Since we don't feel that romantic love that we knew fifteen years ago, I guess divorce would be best," or "Maybe the affair is God's will," or "I have to drink like this because it calms my nerves."

That is why the Bible warns us against being "hardened by the deceitfulness of sin," (Hebrews 3:13). It may not be a so-called "big sin" that deceives you. But whatever impairs the tenderness of your conscience, obscures your sense of God, or diminishes your enthusiasm for spiritual things. That thing is sin to you, however innocent it may be in itself.

Let us prayerfully examine our souls and allow the Spirit to purify us, so that God's power can flow unhindered through our lives.

PRAYER THOUGHTS - Gracious Heavenly Father, we thank You for Your willingness to forgive us our sins in Christ. May we allow the Holy Spirit to convict us of those things which come between ourselves and You. Then, give us victory over those sins that You may be glorified in us.

SHARE YOUR FAITH

SCRIPTURE READING - Acts 1:1-8

In his autobiography *Just As I Am*, Billy Graham tells of a time early in his career when he arrived in a small town to preach a sermon. Wanting to mail a letter, he asked a young boy where the post office was. When the boy told him, Billy thanked him and said, "If you'll come to the Baptist Church this evening, you can hear me telling everyone how to get to heaven."

"I don't think I'll be there," the boy said. "You don't even know your way to the post office."

What are you doing to point others to heaven? I don't know who devised the following IQ test, but it will show you not your intelligence, but your invitation quotient. Take the test and see how you rate at reaching out to others for Christ.

- Have you spoken to anyone this past week concerning what Christ and His Church mean to you?
- Do you often let absent church members know that you have missed them?
- Have you anytime this year invited a newcomer to the community to your church?
- Have you invited any unchurched person recently to come to church

with you?

- Do you seek out new faces in the church services and extend to them a word of welcome?
- Do you take time to greet those who sit near to you before or after services?
- Do you pray regularly for opportunities to reach out to others for the sake of the Gospel?

PRAYER THOUGHTS - Lord, please fire up our zeal to be better witnesses for you.

ARE YOU SPIRITUAL?

SCRIPTURE READING - Galatians 5:16-26

Have you ever asked yourself, "Am I a spiritual person? Do I really love the Lord?" Such questions are usually asked by those who are serious about their faith. They are hard to answer sometimes because of the spiritual civil war which rages within us (see Paul in Romans 7:14-25).

I once heard a preacher who began his message by saying, "I have a confession to make— my heart is desperately wicked." Then he added, "But don't get smug, so is yours." He then read Jeremiah 17:9 which says, "The heart is deceitful above all things and desperately wicked." Most Christians will quickly see themselves in this verse.

On the other hand, Christians often have superficial ways to judge another's spirituality. We may feel spiritually inferior to a believer who is more demonstrative than we are in public worship, who is more precocious in articulating biblical truth, or who spends more time than we do in the so-called spiritual disciplines. Biblically, however, being spiritual is primarily a matter of bearing fruit and living a holy life. Loving Christ is mostly equated with obedience to his commands (see John 14:15 and I John 2:15).

Are we producing the fruit of the Spirit listed in our scripture reading for today? Do we share Christ with others? Are we serving Christ with our time, talents, and earthly treasure? Prayer, Bible study, and worshiping with other believers will help us to be faithful. But the ultimate question is, "Are you walking with Christ?"

PRAYER THOUGHTS - Father, examine my heart and open my eyes to anything that hinders my walk with you. Help me to demonstrate my love for you by humble obedience to your commands.

PRAYING FOR OUR LEADERS

SCRIPTURE READING - I Timothy 2:1-4

We will not always be pleased with our leaders or agree with all their decisions, but God still commands that we pray for them. Here is a prayer I have often prayed on behalf of our nation's leaders.

"Heavenly Father, I thank you for the blessings and freedoms we enjoy as Americans. I pray that you would be with our leaders (our President and his administration, mayors, governors, senators, congressmen, judges, military and law enforcement officials, business leaders, educators, leaders in science, medicine and industry, those who control our news and entertainment media, church and religious leaders). Please give our leaders wisdom to lead us in foreign and domestic affairs, economically and militarily, and above all morally and spiritually. I pray for a great spiritual awakening in this country, that the gospel of Jesus Christ might spread mightily around this nation and throughout the world.

"Be with all of our leaders, local, state, national and worldwide. May many come to place their faith in Christ and may they make their decisions prayerfully, realizing their first responsibility is to You. Help us to encourage additional competent leaders who are truly Christian to run for office or seek high places of leadership. We ask all these favors in the powerful name of Jesus, Amen."

PRAYER THOUGHTS - Almighty God, we acknowledge that You are sovereign over the entire universe. May we never forget that little of lasting good will happen unless we ask You for it in prayer.

BAPTISM – A TEST OF FAITH

SCRIPTURE READING - Acts 8:12-13; 18:8

A common misconception today is that believing in Jesus means that God automatically accepts you. However, God never has accepted human beings on their own terms, but rather exclusively on His own terms and conditions. You see, belief takes place in the heart of the sinner, but forgiveness takes place in the heart of God. Faith in Christ and repentance from sin change your heart, but confession of faith and baptism change your state.

We should not be surprised that God asks us to do something unusual (like being baptized), in order to receive salvation. God has always asked believers to do things which did not appeal to human reason in order to test their faith. He asked Adam and Eve not to eat the forbidden fruit. He commanded Noah to build an ark. He asked Abraham to sacrifice Isaac and submit to circumcision. Jesus asked the rich young ruler to sell all he had and give it to the poor. He ordered the blind man on whose eyes he put the clay to go wash in the Pool of Siloam. He commanded ten lepers who still had leprosy to go show themselves to the priest. Those who obeyed these commands received God's blessings.

What does getting immersed in water have to do with salvation? It is a test of your faith. Repentant believers who obey this command are promised the forgiveness of sins and gift of the Holy Spirit, (Acts 2:38).

PRAYER THOUGHTS - Dear God, we thank you for the grace and forgiveness that are ours as believers in Christ. We are also grateful that in baptism we can know that we have passed from death to life.

TWO BECOMING ONE

SCRIPTURE READING - Matthew 19:3-6

Modern American culture promotes the idea that sexual purity is for wimps. Even many young people who have grown up in the church see nothing wrong with premarital sex. Either they are ignorant of what the Bible teaches about sexual purity before marriage or they don't care.

Our scripture for today gives the Lord's definition of marriage. "A man will leave his father and mother, be united to his wife, and the two will become one flesh."

To "leave father and mother" means that you are establishing a new family, your closest relative will be your spouse from this day forward. To "cleave" is a commitment to put each other first, second only to God. Nobody and nothing on this earth must come between the two of you. Becoming "one flesh" involves a union of both your wills and your bodies. Notice that the physical bonding comes after the vows of commitment are made.

Biblically, marriage is a union which symbolizes the relationship between Christ and the church, (Ephesians 5:31-32). Becoming "one flesh" describes sexual union, (See also I Corinthians 6:16). Sex is a communication process. The Bible uses the word "know" in regard to sexual intercourse, "Adam knew Eve". Sex is not just a body to body experience. It involves body, soul, and spirit. To see sex as merely physical is to trivialize it. This is done all the time by the world, but Christians should not be deceived by this.

PRAYER THOUGHTS - Almighty God, You have put a high wall around sex and marked it "for man and wife only". Help us to respect Your boundaries, realizing that it is for our own good.

ADVICE FOR THE YOUNG

SCRIPTURE READING - John 15:1-8

Late spring and early summer are exciting times, especially for many of our young people. School days are ending and marriages and/or careers are beginning. One parent summed it up rather well by saying, "This is a happy, sad time of the year. I have a son graduating from high school in May and a daughter getting married in June."

We are happy to see young people graduate and move into adulthood. We are happy to see young lives join in marriage and begin their own homes. But there is a tinge of sadness in knowing that many of them will leave the area and we will see them less often.

It is important that we pray for those who are in their teens and twenties. This is a period of momentous challenges and weighty decisions. A whole world of possibilities lies before young people today. They need divine wisdom as they make choices concerning education, vocation, marriage, friendships, lifestyle, etc.

To young people I say, "There are a lot of different philosophies of life out there competing for your allegiance. Some will tell you, 'follow the money.' Others say, 'If it feels good, do it.' Still others urge you to find out what works for you and don't let anybody talk you out of it."

I would point you to Christ. Jesus said, "I am the way and the truth and the life. No one comes to the Father except by me," (John 14:6). He did not say he knew the way. He said I AM the way. He did not say he knew something about the truth. He said HE IS the truth. He did not say I can tell you about life. He said I AM the life. Follow him and he will give you meaning and fulfillment in this world and eternal life in the age to come.

PRAYER THOUGHTS - Father, help us to follow in the footsteps of Your Son in our youth, mid-life, and into old age. May we never forget that apart from Him we can do nothing.

GRACE AND EVANGELISM

SCRIPTURE READING - Ephesians 6:10-17

Our scripture for today discusses the spiritual armor we need as Christians. For our purpose here, we will focus on "the helmet of salvation." The helmet protects the Christian soldier's head. In other words, salvation changes the way you think. When you realize that you are saved by God's grace, that greatly influences your outlook on life.

Why do we need the helmet of salvation? Because the devil wants to mess up our heads. If you can hit a soldier on the head, you can knock him out. The devil does this by trying to sow doubt in our minds. Satan is the accuser of the saints. He wants us to doubt our salvation.

This has a profound impact on your evangelism. When you know you are saved, you are excited about your faith. You have greater zeal to spread the Good News. Only by receiving God's grace can you be motivated to pass it on to others.

On the other hand, you cannot do evangelism bare-headed (without the helmet of salvation). If you doubt your salvation, you will have little energy to evangelize. Remember Ephesians 2:8 which says, "By grace you have been saved," not "by grace you might be saved," (see also I John 5:13).

PRAYER THOUGHTS - Lord, we thank you for your great salvation. Forgive us when we take it for granted and give us the courage to share it with others.

LEARNING TO BE CONTENT

SCRIPTURE READING - Philippians 4:10-13

"Humpty Dumpty sat on a wall. Humpty Dumpty had a great fall. All the king's horses and all the king's men couldn't put Humpty Dumpty together again."

Have you ever felt like Humpty Dumpty? Things are such a mess, you don't see how they will ever work out or perhaps you are merely experiencing an underlying sense of disillusionment and discontentment.

Paul said in Philippians 4:11, "I have learned to be content whatever my circumstances."

Paul didn't just grit his teeth and endure difficult situations. Neither did he always like the circumstances in which he found himself. Rather, Paul discovered that God gives you whatever you need to get through your present situation. This gave Paul peace of mind.

We should be encouraged by the fact that Paul said, "I have learned to be content." In other words, Paul said, "I wasn't always that way. I had to learn it through experience." He grew into it as a believer and so can we.

A normal part of life involves enduring unfulfilled expectations; yet we can be content whatever our circumstances. That does not mean we say, "I like what's happening to me." But it does mean that we can say by faith, "God will give me peace and joy anyhow."

PRAYER THOUGHTS - Lord, we rejoice that although this world is broken, you are preparing us for a perfect eternity. Help us to cope with the trials of this life, realizing that they are only temporary setbacks.

FOCUS ON YOUR ATTITUDE

SCRIPTURE READING - Jeremiah 29:11-13

Jeremiah 29:11 is, for many, a favorite Bible promise. It speaks about hope for the future based on God's plans to prosper us, not to harm us. However, like most Bible promises, it is conditional. Jeremiah says that we must call upon God and seek Him with our whole heart. Half-hearted effort to do God's will won't take us to the "promised land."

We human beings tend to be self-centered and narcissistic. It is easy for our walk with God to shift until it is no longer about God. Many have taken God's truths and twisted them into selfish pursuits. When that happens, promises like the one in today's scripture are taken for granted. We mistakenly assume that God will cater to us regardless of our degree of commitment.

Consider this true story. One year our church chose Jeremiah 29:11 as the theme verse for a building fund campaign. When the printer showed us the proof for our banner, it contained a typo. Instead of Jeremiah 29:11, he had put Jeremiah 25:11. Jeremiah 25:11 says, "This whole country will become a desolate wasteland, and these nations will serve the king of Babylon seventy years."

One number makes the difference between a "desolate wasteland" and a "prosperous future". Our attitude toward God makes the same difference when it comes to receiving our spiritual inheritance.

PRAYER THOUGHTS - Lord, how awesome it is to realize how much You want to bless and use our lives for Your glory. Help us to set aside those things which take our focus away from full surrender to Your work and Your will.

PARENTING

SCRIPTURE READING - Deuteronomy 6:4-9

Being a parent is one of the most challenging tasks on earth. It can also be very rewarding. Some parents have a child who stood on their shoulders and achieved far more than Mom or Dad. That is a real joy. Other stories are not as happy, but that is the risk we take when we conceive.

Parenthood is serious business. We can enjoy our children, but we are not called by God to be their buddies. Our task is to train them and discipline them to become men and women of God. Training involves rules and regulations with rewards and punishment. The word "discipline" literally means "to make a disciple of". We ought to be able to say with the apostle Paul, "Follow my example, as I follow the example of Christ," (I Corinthians 11:1).

Our scripture reading points out that we must be devoted to God's Word and with pleasing Him and teach our children to do the same. Results are not guaranteed in parenting. Adam and Eve had a perfect Father, yet they rebelled. All we can do is sow the seed and pray for a good harvest.

PRAYER THOUGHTS - Heavenly Father, thank You for loving us enough to both encourage and correct us. Give us wisdom and courage to follow Your example with our own children.

THE DANGER OF FALLING AWAY

SCRIPTURE READING - Hebrews 6:4-6; 2 Peter 2:20-22

The New Testament is clear that believers in Christ can be secure in their salvation. Romans 8:1 says that there is "no condemnation for those who are in Christ Jesus". This promise is sometimes hard to believe because we, as Christians, sometimes backslide into sin and our hearts condemn us. When that happens, we are told to confess our sins so that God may "purify us from all unrighteousness," (John 1:9).

At the same time, the Bible warns us about the possibility of a believer backsliding so far from God that he or she becomes an apostate. The word "apostasy" sounds like the Greek word used in Hebrews 6:6 which is translated "fall away." It can also mean "to remove oneself" or "to resign". In other words, if we are careless or rebellious or apathetic spiritually, we can, in effect, resign as a believer in Christ. The writer of Hebrews says that we can reach a point where we are incapable of repentance.

Jesus said of His followers in John 10:28, "no one can snatch them out of my hand". I believe that with all my heart. As long as I hold onto Jesus, nobody and nothing can separate me from Him. But what if I voluntarily choose to leave His hand? What if I "resign" as a disciple, never to repent and return to His side? That is where our scriptures for today become relevant and frightening. The Lord will not hold us hostage against our will. Let us make sure we do not lose our faith. Then we can rest in blessed assurance.

PRAYER THOUGHTS - Lord, may we never take for granted Your grace by which we are saved. Help us to stay in fellowship with You so that our hearts will not grow cold.

GOD AND YOUR MONEY

SCRIPTURE READING - Matthew 19:16-26

The young man in our scripture today was a good, moral person and he had a lot of money. Jesus did not try to get his money, but the Lord confronted him. Jesus basically said, "You have a money problem. You have a love for and trust in money," and Jesus said, "Until you squash that, you can't be a Christian."

The problem with the story of the rich young ruler is that we do not think of ourselves as being rich. The way we usually think is that a rich person is someone who has more than we do. Biblically speaking, however, anyone who has more than basic food, clothing, and shelter is considered rich enough to be generous with the needy.

If God has blessed us with our needs plus some luxuries, these blessings can easily distract us from God and eternal values and all the things that are really important.

Jesus said, "You cannot serve both God and money," (Matthew 6:24). The rich young ruler had to make a choice and so do we. Giving money to God is important, but He is interested in the whole person. Matthew 6:33 says, "Seek first the kingdom of God," and God will take care of your needs. Do not let money, luxuries, or keeping up with your friends cause you to put God in second place.

PRAYER THOUGHTS - Lord, give us wisdom never to make money and what it can buy more important than You.

ENDURING EVIL AND SUFFERING

SCRIPTURE READING - John 3:16; Romans 8:28

The first three chapters of the book of Genesis tell us that God created the earth to be perfect. The first human beings were created innocent, but with the power of choice. God gave us free choice because He wanted us to love Him. Love that is not freely given is not love. Unfortunately, we often use our free choice to reject the good which God offers us. When that happens, innocent people are often hurt along with the guilty. All sin is a result of lies, questioning whether God loves us or knows what is best for us.

Also, in Genesis chapter three, we learn that this world itself is under a curse because of human sin. The Bible tells us that because of this curse, natural disasters must come (sickness, accidents, storms, etc.). God never promises to keep us from such things, but to be with us through them. Since sin has entered the world, there will be evidence of Satan's influence.

The two verses in our scripture reading for today show that God blesses the believer in spite of hardships in this world and will give us eternal life in the world to come. With these promises in view, all the trials of this life seem rather insignificant, don't they?

PRAYER THOUGHTS - Gracious Father, help us to keep looking up when all about us would drag us down. May we never forget your promises when our faith grows weak.

MAINTAINING A HEALTHY MARRIAGE

SCRIPTURE READING - Philippians 2:1-4

One of the most important skills to have in maintaining a healthy marriage is to know how to cope with conflict. People Magazine once conducted a reader's opinion poll on how to respond to irreconcilable differences in marriage. The results were as follows: 37% said divorce or give it up, 34% said you should try to rekindle affection, 16% suggested suffering quietly, and 9% advocated taking a lover on the side and staying together anyway.

In other words, two-thirds of those who responded believe a weak marriage is to be either ended or merely endured. Are the remaining one-third who think it is possible for things to improve just naïve? I don't think so. I have seen too many sick marriages get well again. It must begin with a commitment by both of the parties to rebuild the relationship, plus following some basic rules for discussing sources of conflict. For example:

- Express all irritations and annoyances in a loving, specific, and positive way.
- Do not attack the other person, exaggerate their faults, or toss in their past failures. Stick to the issue at hand.
- Control the emotional level and intensity of arguments (no yelling, uncontrollable anger, or hurtful remarks).

- Do not let the sun go down on your anger or run away from each other during an argument.
- Do not interrupt each other. Concentrate on what the other person is saying rather than thinking up a defense.
- If something is important enough for one person to discuss, it is that important for the other person.

PRAYER THOUGHTS - Gracious Lord, we lift up to You broken marriages and hurting families. May we humble ourselves before You and our spouses that relationships may be healed.

SHARE THE GOSPEL

SCRIPTURE READING - Matthew 28:18-20

Our scripture for today has been called "The Great Commission". Our Lord and Savior Jesus Christ had been given all authority in heaven and on earth. He sends His followers out to make disciples, baptize them, and teach them all the things our Lord has commanded. This is an awesome task, but we are not alone. As we obey this commission, He is with us "always, to the very end of the age".

In spite of the emphasis Jesus placed on making disciples, most Christians find it difficult to share the gospel. A majority of churches tend to be focused on input rather than outreach. It is easier for believers to talk to each other about the faith rather than trying to reach unbelievers. We need to be constantly reminded that the church is not here primarily for its current members. It is here for those who are still outside of Christ.

Jesus told the parable of a shepherd who left his flock of ninety-nine sheep behind in order to find the one which was lost, (Luke 15:1-7). Likewise, we must prefer to seek the lost rather than to satisfy the saved.

PRAYER THOUGHTS - Heavenly Father, please open our eyes to see those around us who need Christ and give us the courage to share the gospel with them.

FINDING SPIRITUAL STRENGTH

SCRIPTURE READING - Isaiah 7:3-9

Our scripture for today concludes with the words, "If you do not stand firm in your faith, you will not stand at all."

Faith both motivates us and sustains us. It motivates to action, because real faith is not just something you say or even feel. Nor is faith merely something you think or believe. Real faith is something you do. James 2:17 says that "...faith by itself, if it is not accompanied by action, is dead."

Then, faith also sustains us. If our confidence is not in God, we will sooner or later hit a wall. If we put our hope in our own strength, we will someday get tired and weak. Then the enemy will move in for the kill. If we trust in our own wisdom, we will eventually run out of answers. If our confidence is in family and friends, they will not always be there when we need them. We must look to Him who never fails, who always keeps His promises, who cannot lie, and who stays the same "yesterday, today and forever," (Hebrews 13:8).

A faith that is genuine will help us to stand firm for God and against the Evil One. Our source of spiritual strength is found in believing God's Word, obeying His commands and trusting His promises.

PRAYER THOUGHTS - Lord, we know that You call upon us to live by faith. Help us to remember that faith in You is the victory that overcomes the world.

WHAT IS YOUR FOCUS?

SCRIPTURE READING - Matthew 23:1-15

A speaker at a conference for preachers asked this question: "In your preaching, are you more like a ballet dancer or a stripper?" That got everyone's attention! He then explained that a ballerina seeks to focus attention on the story while a stripper draws attention to herself."

The lesson was obvious. Our task in preaching, or whatever our ministry in the Kingdom may be, is to bring glory to Christ, not ourselves. But while we may mentally acknowledge that principle in theory, we may forget it in actual practice.

Jesus sternly denounced the scribes and Pharisees whose service to God was often nothing more than an ego trip. The Lord said, "Unless your righteousness exceeds that of the Pharisees and teachers of the law, you will never enter the Kingdom of Heaven," (Matthew 5:20).

In Matthew 6:5 and 16, Jesus taught that those who do religious acts to impress others have received their reward in full. I don't know about you, but I want to receive my reward in Glory. In order to do that, we must give all honor to God. As one wise person said, "Where you go hereafter depends on what you are going after here."

PRAYER THOUGHTS - Father, we confess that the only righteousness we possess is a gift of your grace to those of us who believe in Christ. Help us to live and give as grateful servants in your Kingdom.

EXCUSES

SCRIPTURE READING - Luke 14:15-24

When I was a boy, my father preached a sermon entitled "Eating Soup with a Hatchet". He announced the sermon title a couple weeks in advance and asked people to guess what the sermon would be about. Nobody figured it out. He began his message with this story. A man had a neighbor who frequently borrowed things which he never returned. One day the son was in the yard when the neighbor came over. The neighbor wanted to borrow a hatchet, so the son went and asked his father. The father said, "Tell him he can't have my hatchet today because I'm eating soup with it."

The son said, "You never eat soup with a hatchet."

The father replied, "If you don't want to do something, one excuse is as good as another."

You would be amazed to hear some of the excuses I have heard people give. A Presbyterian minister wrote a satirical piece concerning the time-worn excuses people give for not attending church. It is entitled "Ten Reasons Why I Never Wash". Here are some of them:

"I was made to wash as a child."

"People who wash are hypocrites, they think they are cleaner than other people."

"I used to wash, but it got boring so I quit."

"There are so many different kinds of soap, I could never decide which one was right."

"I still wash on special occasions like Christmas and Easter."

"None of my friends wash."

"I'm still young. When I'm older and have got a bit dirtier, I might start washing."

"People who make soap are only after your money."

If excuses like these sound phony to us, imagine what God thinks of them?

PRAYER THOUGHTS - Lord, thank you for laying down your life for us. Forgive us when we forget and put anything ahead of you.

FLEE FROM PRIDE

SCRIPTURE READING - Isaiah 14:12-15

In his prophecy against Babylon, Isaiah speaks of the fall of the devil. It was pride that brought Satan down. Pride also led to the fall of humanity into sin and death. The Evil One persuaded Eve that if she ate the forbidden fruit, she would "be like God," (Genesis 3:5).

Indeed, pride is at the root of all sin when we put ourselves on the throne in place of God. We can do this by either exalting or debasing ourselves. The self-exalted delude themselves into believing they do not need God. Others have an inverted pride and see themselves as inferior. They say, in effect, "God left me out of His blessings." This brings them a lot of sympathy which is a backward way of putting themselves on the throne.

Pride also does untold damage to human relationships. It causes unhealthy competition, sensitive egos, power struggles, hurt feelings, damaged friendships, fractured families, split churches, and even wars.

Ultimately, pride keeps people unsaved and without hope. Many refuse to believe in God's judgment because they want to be in control. They even spurn God's grace, since accepting it means they must give God their allegiance in gratitude. Don't let pride separate you from God eternally!

PRAYER THOUGHTS - Heavenly Father, may we never allow our foolish pride to separate us from your love, grace and forgiveness in Christ.

AMBASSADORS FOR CHRIST

SCRIPTURE READING - 2 Corinthians 5:17-20

Russ Blowers (last name rhymes with "flowers") was an outstanding preacher who ministered with a large church in Indianapolis for nearly forty years. Knowing he would be asked to share his profession at a Rotary Club meeting, he came up with the following statement:

"Hi, I'm Russ Blowers. I am with a global enterprise. We have branches in every country in the world. We have representatives in nearly every parliament and boardroom on earth. We're into motivation and behavior alteration. We run hospitals, feeding stations, crisis pregnancy centers, universities, publishing houses, and nursing homes. We care for our clients from birth to death. We are into life insurance and fire insurance. We perform spiritual heart transplants. Our original Organizer owns all the real estate on earth plus an assortment of galaxies and constellations. He knows everything and lives everywhere. Our product is free for the taking. Our C. E. O. was born in a hick-town, worked as a carpenter, didn't own a home, was misunderstood by his family and hated by his enemies, walked on water, was condemned to death without a trial, and arose from the dead. I talk with him every day."

Every one of us as Christians ought to be able to make the same statement. What a tremendous calling is ours as ambassadors for Christ. As we share our faith, hearts are touched and lives are changed. Furthermore, Jesus promises to be with us always "to the very end of the age," (Matthew 28:20).

PRAYER THOUGHTS - Lord, we thank you for your great salvation. Give us courage to be your witnesses to a lost and dying world.

GUARDING THE EYE-GATE

SCRIPTURE READING - Psalm 101:2-3

The old children's song says, "Be careful little eyes what you see. Be careful little ears what you hear." The implication is that even a child has some control over the images and information which absorbs his or her attention. How much more responsible should we be as adults? We should "set no vile thing before our eyes," (Psalm 101:3).

This may refer to impure entertainment, pornography, or even a lustful look. Jesus warned that it is not good enough to avoid adultery. We must also abstain from burning with desire for someone other than our spouse, (Matthew 5:27-28).

Pornography, for example, is designed to inflame lust. The word "pornography" literally means "pictures of prostitutes". The production and dissemination of porn is big business. Not all porn is pictures. Much of it is prose which evokes erotic desires. Many Christians who feed on this material claim that it does no harm. To excuse this as innocent, however, is naïve. If good behavior is influenced by uplifting media, wouldn't bad conduct be influenced by material which is pornographic? Ideas and images spur action. That is why businesses spend so much on advertising.

We must guard carefully that which enters our mind through the eye-gate. Some other scriptures to consider on this subject are Job 31:1, Colossians 3:1-4, Ephesians 5:8-12, Philippians 4:8, and Galatians 5:24.

PRAYER THOUGHTS - "May the words of my mouth and the meditation of my heart be pleasing in your sight, O Lord, my Rock and my Redeemer," (Psalm 19:14).

WHICH ONE?

SCRIPTURE READING - Isaiah 52:7

Once upon a time there were three Christian men who were good friends named Clyde Congenial, Calvin Controversy, and Carl Cool. Although they shared their faith and friendship in common, they had important differences.

Clyde Congenial's motto seemed to be, "Don't make waves, make friends." This carried over into his Christian witness. He sought to charm people into the kingdom. If he sensed the least discomfort in a prospect, he would start talking about the weather or some other subject that was nice and neutral. Consequently, he never became the dynamic soul winner he wanted to be.

Calvin Controversy was just the opposite of his friend Clyde. His motto was, "There is no progress without controversy." Calvin loved religious debates and usually won. His problem was that he loved controversy more than he loved people. People sensed this and were not impressed by either his logic or his faith.

Finally, there was Carl Cool. This guy had a keen sense of timing. He waited patiently for the right time to speak up for Christ. He also knew the right time to be quiet, but he realized that a person was often irritated by the conviction of the Holy Spirit and that such irritation could be a good sign to follow through. Carl's motto came straight from the Bible, "A good word spoken at the right time, how good it is!" (Proverbs 15:23).

You will find these three types of individuals in any church family. Which one most resembles you?

PRAYER THOUGHTS - Heavenly Father, thank you for giving us a life-changing Gospel to share. Give us holy boldness to seize those moments when others may be open to Your Word.

INTEGRITY

SCRIPTURE READING - Matthew 5:33-37

Integrity comes from the word "integrated". It means that your beliefs and your behavior match up. If a person has integrity, you can take them at their word. If they say "yes," they mean "yes." If they say "no," they mean "no," (Matthew 5:37). People of integrity keep the promises and commitments they make.

Sadly, integrity is in short supply in our society today. What Paul said about the citizens of Crete in Titus 1:12 could be said of Americans: "Cretans are always liars."

Nevertheless, unbelievers expect Christians to maintain a higher standard than most. Unfortunately, those who profess faith in Christ sometimes fail to meet God's standards when it comes to their business ethics or honesty in paying taxes, etc.

The words of Christ in today's scripture are not merely a condemnation of swearing. Jesus is also saying that it is unnecessary to make a promise with an oath attached if you are a person of integrity. Dishonesty and deceptive speech are a heart problem and the Lord came to change hearts. People of God are people of integrity.

PRAYER THOUGHTS - Heavenly Father, we confess that we cannot have true integrity without you. Help us to show the world through our character that we have been made whole in Christ.

THE TRUE NATURE OF WORSHIP

SCRIPTURE READING - John 4:19-24

In our scripture reading, Jesus tells the Samaritan woman that location is irrelevant to worship. What matters is our desire to honor and praise the Lord (our "spirit') and our attitude of submission to God's Word (the "truth"). Whether we are in a public assembly or by ourselves, worship is a personal and spiritual communion with God.

In the New Testament, public worship included such things as instruction in God's Word, fellowship, the Lord's Supper, prayer, musical praise, and receiving an offering, (see Acts 2:42; 20:7; I Corinthians 16:1-2; Ephesians 5:19 and Colossians 3:16).

Worship may be a scheduled activity with others or when you have your personal devotions. Sometimes worship may occur spontaneously as when you see a beautiful sunset, hold a baby in your arms, or thank God for answered prayer.

God does expect us to worship Him with other believers through prescribed ritual. However, scheduling worship does not guarantee that worship is taking place. True worship should happen every day for sincere believers. Worship is frequent and spontaneous for those who love God and are grateful for all He has given us.

PRAYER THOUGHTS - Heavenly Father, You are awesome and majestic, yet full of holiness and compassion. Help us always to give You the glory due Your name.

PUT "GO" BACK IN THE CHURCH

SCRIPTURE READING - Matthew 28:16-20

Jesus wants the church to be on the go. In today's scripture Jesus told us to "go and make disciples". Many churches have replaced the word "go" with "come". Instead of going out into the community, they invite people to come to church.

Where would Jesus go if He came to our community for several days? He would probably go where good church members are told not to go. Jesus said, "I have not come to call the righteous, but sinners," (Mark 2:17). So we need to ask ourselves, "How many groups do we have that target un-churched people? What incentives are we giving Christians to contact unbelievers?"

Our scripture reading is called the Great Commission. It reveals that the purpose of the church is to reach the lost for Christ and then teach them to be disciples. We need to examine each ministry and activity of the church to determine if they are fulfilling this purpose. Programs which are not fulfilling the purpose of the church must be cut. This is painful and people will be upset, but it needs to happen in most churches.

PRAYER THOUGHTS - Lord of the harvest, open our eyes to see those around us who are without Christ and without hope. Give us wisdom and courage to reach out to them with the Gospel.

KEEPING THE CROSS CENTRAL

SCRIPTURE READING - Galatians 6:14; I Corinthians 2:2

When the Apostle Paul went to that highly intellectual city of Corinth, he could have impressed them with his great learning. Instead, Paul focused on one subject, the cross of Christ. Why? Because the cross reveals both human sin and God's love.

The cross is central to the Gospel because of the magnetism of the one who died there. Jesus said, "And I, when I am lifted up from the earth, will draw all people to myself," (John 12:32). Jesus was speaking of his death on the cross.

The Old Covenant taught that "apart from the shedding of blood there is no forgiveness of sins," (Hebrews 9:22). God kept that rule even when it cost Him the blood of His only begotten Son. Thus the cross reveals the love and grace of both the Father and the Son.

But the cross also reveals the reality of our sin. That is why the world is offended by it. I Corinthians 1:23 says the cross is a stumbling block to the Jews and foolishness to the Gentiles. Many do not realize that the answer to the world's problems is at the foot of the cross. The human predicament is sin and guilt and fear of death. So, at the cross "God made him who had no sin to be sin for us, so that in him we might become the righteousness of God," (2 Corinthians 5:21).

PRAYER THOUGHTS - Father, give us courage to tell others the good news of Christ crucified, knowing that it is the only hope for this lost and dying world.

BEING GOOD ENOUGH
ISN'T GOOD ENOUGH

SCRIPTURE READING - Galatians 2:17-21

Many unbelievers, and even Christians, believe mistakenly that we are saved by living a good life. A question I have used often when talking to people about salvation is, "If you were to stand before God and He were to ask you, 'Why should I let you into My heaven?' What would you say?"

The vast majority says something like, "Even though I am not perfect, I have tried to live a good life."

If that is all it takes to get into heaven, then why did Jesus have to die on the cross for our sins? Paul says in our scripture today. "....if righteousness could be gained through the law, Christ died for nothing." The truth is that apart from faith in Christ as our Savior, all of our good works will not save us from eternal condemnation. Ephesians 2:8-9 sums it up: "For it is by grace you have been saved through faith; and this not from yourselves, it is the gift of God; not by works, so that no one can boast."

Don't trust in yourself for salvation. Being good enough isn't good enough. Only by putting your faith in Christ as your Savior can you be certain of going to heaven.

You can accept God's salvation in Christ by believing in Jesus as your Lord and Savior, repenting of your sins, confessing your faith in Christ, and being buried with Him in the waters of baptism, (See Acts 2:36-38; Romans 10:9-10).

PRAYER THOUGHTS - Lord, we thank you for your redemptive work on the cross. May all who read these words avail themselves of that salvation before it is too late.

WHY IS GOD JEALOUS?

SCRIPTURE READING - Exodus 20:1-6

One lady said that she stopped being a Christian when she learned that God was a jealous God. She said, "I can't worship a God who is jealous of me."

She missed the point of what it means for God to be jealous. It does not mean that God is jealous (or envious) of us, who we are, or what we have. That would be absurd for the Sovereign Being of the universe to envy us. Rather, God is jealous for our devotion, love, worship, and obedience. He will not transfer to another the honor that is due to Himself, nor tolerate our worship of any other god.

God spoke through Isaiah, "I am the Lord; that is my name! I will not give my glory to another or my praise to idols," (Isaiah 42:8). The first four of the Ten Commandments focus on our devotion to God. He is the only true and living God, we are not to worship idols, we must not misuse His name, and we should worship Him on His designated day. Under the Old Covenant, that was the Sabbath (seventh day of the week). Under the New Covenant, it is the Lord's Day (first day of the week).

God knows that if we give our ultimate allegiance to anyone but Him, we are in danger of going astray from the path of righteousness. He wants what is best for us and He alone can assure that we will gain the prize of eternal life.

PRAYER THOUGHTS - Loving Father, please forgive us those times when we are distracted from following You alone. Thank you for this reminder that faithfulness to you must be our top priority.

HOW TO BE FILLED WITH THE HOLY SPIRIT

SCRIPTURE READING - Ephesians 5:15-20

Our scripture for today exhorts us to be filled with the Holy Spirit, (v. 18). The gift of the Holy Spirit is promised to repentant believers when they are buried with Christ in baptism, (Acts 2:38-39). Once you have the Holy Spirit however, your greatest challenge is to let the Holy Spirit have more of you. That is what is meant by being filled with the Holy Spirit.

How do we go about doing that? Following are four steps which have been helpful to me and many others. These steps are scriptural, powerful and effective:

> **CLEAR YOUR CONSCIENCE** WITH GOD. Do you have any sins standing between you and the Lord? Confess them to God and claim forgiveness. I John 1:9 says, "If we confess our sins, he is faithful and just and will forgive us our sins and purify us from all unrighteousness."
>
> **CHOOSE AGAINST YOURSELF.** Resolve to do what pleases the Lord from this day forward. Truly repent of your sins and determine to choose God's way, (See Luke 9:23-24).
>
> **ALLOW CHRIST TO LIVE IN YOU.** Choose the will of God instead of your own will, in every detail, for the rest

of your life. That is tough, but with the power of the Spirit, it is not impossible, (See Galatians 2:20).

CROWN JESUS CHRIST AS THE LORD OF YOUR LIFE. Revelation 17:14 says, "They will make war against the Lamb, but the Lamb will overcome them because he is Lord of Lords and King of Kings; and with him will be his called, chosen and faithful followers."

PRAYER THOUGHTS - Almighty God, remind us daily of your power to make our lives more beautiful and useful. May we allow your Spirit within us to lead us in the way everlasting.

THE SOURCE OF OUR HOPE

SCRIPTURE READING - I Thessalonians 4:13-18

A missionary to Asia reported on the persecution of Christians in China. The government only recognizes those churches which submit to certain restrictions. They prohibit education programs for children like Sunday School and nobody under twenty-one may be baptized. The communist government also controls the ordination and assigning of ministers.

But the most interesting limitation is that only one restriction was made on doctrine. The only thing the Chinese government will not permit official churches to teach is "the second coming of Christ."

Why do the government leaders feel so threatened by this doctrine? Perhaps because of the hope factor. Communists do not want their citizens to put their hope in anything but the government. They do not want their people to believe in the One who will overthrow human authority and reign over His own Kingdom forever.

Those of us who still have the freedom to teach that Christ is returning often neglect to do so. This teaching, which the Chinese government considers the most dangerous doctrine of Christianity, is only dangerous to unbelievers. To us who believe, it is our cherished hope!

PRAYER THOUGHTS - Precious Lord, we thank You for conquering death for us by Your victorious resurrection. We trust Your promise to raise up believers to eternal life on that Day.

PREPARE FOR THE NEW YEAR

SCRIPTURE READING - Philippians 3:12-14

What personal goals do you have for the upcoming year? I learned to be a goal-setter when I was a teenager. I admired singer Pat Boone who was also a spokesman for Christianity. He wrote a book for teenagers called *Twixt Twelve and Twenty*. Avis Callison, my Sunday School teacher, gave me the book as a birthday present. I was a freshman in high school. I read the book several times and it changed my life.

One thing Boone suggested was to set goals for yourself in six different areas of life. The categories were spiritual, mental, social, physical, financial, and work.

To grow spiritually, I began to read the Bible and pray every day. For mental growth, I made a list of good books and started to read them. Socially, I began to reach out more to develop some solid friendships. Physically, I started doing a regimen of daily calisthenics. A financial goal was to save money for college and a college car. Goals for my life's work became more focused when I decided I wanted to be a preacher. My parents taught me a good work ethic and I started delivering newspapers when I was ten years old. After that, I always had some kind of paying job.

The most productive people are goal-setters. The Apostle Paul often compared life to a race. Are you running the race of life or are you just running laps? If you do not have goals, you are probably just drifting. Pray about what God would have you do in the New Year. Then set some specific goals. You will be glad you did.

PRAYER THOUGHTS - Dear God, we know not what the future holds, but we know You hold the future. Give us guidance to set goals that will fulfill Your purpose in our lives.

EASTER HOPE

SCRIPTURE READING - Romans 8:9-11

If there is anything this world needs more of now, it is hope. That is why we need Easter more than ever. The older I get, the more I realize that it is easy for me to become cynical about life. A cynic tends to doubt the sincerity and good intentions of others. He or she becomes distrustful of human nature and pessimistic about the future.

A part of the problem is that I have seen many changes in this country during my lifetime and many of them have been for the worse. I grew up in the forties and fifties. As a young adult in the sixties, I saw America's values go down the tubes. Our society quickly descended into a cesspool of sexual promiscuity, drug abuse, abortion on demand, legalized gambling, rampant blasphemy, and a flood of pornography. The moral decline has continued from that point with few interruptions.

In spite of that, however, I do not despair because we serve a risen Savior. In a world full of empty promises, we have resurrection power. We can rise above this mess on a daily basis and ultimately will be lifted out of this veil of tears. Hearts are still touched and lives are still being changed by the message of hope Christ has given us!

PRAYER THOUGHTS - Heavenly Father, we thank you for a risen Savior. Help us to claim the victory that is ours both for time and eternity

BECAUSE OF EASTER

SCRIPTURE READING - I Corinthians 15:12-19

Because of Easter, the Lord's Supper has great meaning! Matthew 26:26-29 records the institution of the Lord's Supper by Jesus Christ with His disciples. In this passage, Jesus tells them to eat the bread which is His body and drink the cup which is His blood, shed for the forgiveness of sins. In verse 29, Jesus says, "I shall not again drink of the fruit of the vine from now on until I drink it new with you in my Father's Kingdom."

The body and blood of Christ have power to atone for our sins because Jesus rose from the dead. In verse 17 of today's scripture, Paul said that if Christ has not been raised "you are still in your sins." Without Easter there is no salvation, no New Covenant, and no such thing as eternal life. Baptism has no meaning, the Lord's Supper makes no sense, your faith in Christ is worthless, and the church is just another organization of do-gooders and nothing more.

Furthermore, in the account from Matthew quoted above, Jesus said that the Lord's Supper is also a prediction of His second coming. Someday after He returns, we will have communion with Him in His eternal kingdom. This, too, only has meaning because of Easter Sunday. If Jesus did not rise from the dead, then He did not ascend back into heaven to prepare a place for us. If He is not in heaven, He will not be coming back for us. We have no hope whatsoever beyond this life.

Meditate about the infinite importance of Christ's resurrection as you prepare to celebrate this Easter season.

PRAYER THOUGHTS - Dear Lord, we thank you for resurrection power which makes possible the gift of eternal life. May we rejoice in our salvation and share the Good News with others.

A MOTHER'S DAY TRIBUTE

SCRIPTURE READING - Proverbs 31:26-31

My mother and I had similar personalities – fun-loving and perfectionistic. She was gifted at sensing what people were feeling. Mom was also a talented musician and loved being with people.

One of the greatest gifts my mother gave me was reverence for God and a sensitive conscience. She said, "The only thing that will keep you on the 'straight and narrow' is the fear of God." When I started dating, she said, "It doesn't take two bad people to get into trouble, but two good people in a bad situation."

Mom was an enthusiastic student of the Bible and personal evangelist. She was unafraid to share her faith, but backed off if somebody was resistant. One of her favorite sayings was, "People convinced against their will are of the same opinion still." Jesus called it "throwing your pearls to the pigs," (Matthew 7:6).

Mom loved to laugh. For many years she was my main source for jokes. She believed that faith in God and a sense of humor will get you through anything.

"Charm is deceptive, and beauty is fleeting; but a woman who fears the Lord is to be praised," (Proverbs 31:30).

PRAYER THOUGHTS - Lord God, we know that you bless those who have godly mothers. Be especially close to those who do not.

A FATHER'S DAY TRIBUTE

SCRIPTURE READING - Proverbs 1:8-9

I am reminded of some of the wise sayings of my earthly father. Dad was never a fancy talker, but he was a practical philosopher on many subjects. Below is a sample of things I remember him saying over the years.

> **ON PREACHING** (Dad was a pastor, too) - Be kind when you preach. Pretend you are at a family reunion and you're speaking to all your aunts, uncles, and cousins.
>
> **ON EDUCATION** - You learn as much from people and life as you do from books, so don't let your education interfere with your learning.
>
> **ON HUMILITY** - The person who asks a question is a fool for five minutes, but the person who does not ask is a fool forever.
>
> **SURVIVING ON CITY STREETS** - Do not speak unless spoken to and don't smart off to anyone.
>
> **DIETING** - Stop eating while you are still a little hungry.
>
> **MATERIAL THINGS** - Baby your possessions and make them last.
>
> **MONEY** - Give God the first ten percent and save the second ten percent.

WORK - Duty comes before pleasure, but take time to play.

HONESTY - Some bosses will leave money lying around just to see if you will take it. Character is what you are when you think nobody is watching.

MARRIAGE - Find a girl with a pleasant disposition who is not spoiled.

MINISTRY - You cannot please everybody, so seek to please God and God's people will be pleased with you.

So, what good memories do you have about your father? If you are fortunate enough to still have him around, remind him of those happy times.

PRAYER THOUGHTS - Lord, we thank you for godly fathers who guide, provide, and protect us. Help us to daily submit to our Heavenly Father who alone can save us.

A THANKSGIVING REMINDER

SCRIPTURE READING - Psalm 95:1-7

In the classic movie, *Shenandoah*, the leading character, played by Jimmy Stewart, opens the film with a prayer of thanksgiving for a meal. He calls the family in, makes the kids sit still, and prays, "Lord, we plowed the field, we planted the field, we harvested the crop. We cooked it and put it on the table. It wouldn't be here if it weren't for our hard work. But we thank you for it anyway. Amen."

We chuckle at the scene, but I suspect Jimmy Stewart's character illustrates the attitude of many church members. God's material blessings are only indirect at best.

As Americans, God has blessed us with a land of freedom and great bounty. The danger is that we may forget the source of these blessings. Consider the following warning Moses gave to ancient Israel.

"When you have eaten and are satisfied, praise the Lord your God for the good land He has given you, or your heart will become proud and you will forget the Lord your God. You may say to yourself, 'My power and the strength of my hands have produced this wealth for me.' But remember the Lord your God, for it is He who gives you the ability to produce wealth," (Deuteronomy 8:10, 14, 17, 18).

Most of us could probably pray the following Thanksgiving Prayer penned by an anonymous writer: "Father, bless us according to our thanklessness, lest Thou bless us according to our thankfulness and we starve."

PRAYER THOUGHTS - Almighty God, we acknowledge that all good things come from your hand. Forgive us for our ingratitude and accept our thanks today.

PONDER THE WONDER

SCRIPTURE READING - Luke 2:1-20

The man was in his sixties, old enough to be retired, but also old enough to know better. He said to me, "I get bored going to church in December because I've heard the Christmas story a hundred times before." I immediately recalled the words from the old hymn "I Love to Tell the Story" which go, "I love to tell the story, for those who know it best, seem hungering and thirsting to hear it like the rest."

May we never lose the wonder of the story of Christ's birth and all the drama and glory of that first Christmas! We have a wonderful faith, and the word "wonderful" simply means to be full of wonder. Every time I think about God becoming man, it boggles my mind. Oh, I can understand it, God became man. A five-year-old kid can repeat that, but it is a wonder!

Then when I think about God dying, crucified on a cross, I stand in wonder at such love and grace. When I think about a hardened sinner becoming a sweet saint, that is the wonder of the Spirit's regenerating power!

Do you ever stand in awe and wonder at a God who can keep track of billions of people, always answers his phone, and can hear everybody's prayers all at once? Then think about the church that has the rich and the poor, the strong and the weak, and people of all races, yet in Christ we have a unity that is stronger than all Hell! I don't know how we are all going to be resurrected on that last day and be received up in the air and united with the Lord, but I believe we will be.

The Christmas season is a great time to ponder the wonder of all that God has done and continues to do for us in Jesus Christ!

PRAYER THOUGHTS - Gracious Father, may we never take for granted your love and mercy that prompted you to send Heaven's best for our worst. Give us wisdom to share this good news not only at Christmas-time, but throughout the year.

A STABLE BABY FOR AN UNSTABLE WORLD

SCRIPTURE READING - Isaiah 9:6-7

Babies are delightful and exciting! We get sentimental about a newborn child and that is one of the charming things about Christmas. What is even more amazing, however, is that we still remember a poor peasant baby born two thousand years ago. His arrival is so significant that all time is counted from the date of his birth.

We should also realize that Jesus would not be remembered today if he had not risen from the dead. It is because of Easter that we celebrate Christmas. If Jesus had died on the cross and stayed dead, we would not even know his name. He would have been just another religious imposter who died a martyr's death.

Many factors hinge on the resurrection of Christ. For example, if Jesus rose from the dead, then there is a Heaven to gain and a Hell to shun. If Jesus rose from the dead, then believers will see their Christian loved ones again in glory. If Jesus rose from the dead, then whatever troubles bother believers today are trivial compared to what awaits them. If Jesus rose from the dead, then Christians should move heaven and earth to tell others about him. If Jesus rose from the dead, then being a Christian is the greatest privilege on earth. If Jesus rose from the dead, then he is coming back for those who love him. If Jesus rose from the dead, then Christmas celebrates the most important birthday in history!

PRAYER THOUGHTS - Lord, we remember your first arrival because you are coming back. Thank you for this blessed hope which enables us to endure this world's uncertainties.

AFTERWORD

Whether you have read this book straight through or read one devotion per day over a period of time, I hope you make it a habit to be daily into God's Word.

Why is this important? Because our souls need to be fed regularly just as our bodies do. Without daily spiritual input, we will end up just drifting in our walk with God. The call of the world plus our fleshly appetites constantly war against the power of the Holy Spirit in guiding us. The Bible keeps reminding us of who we are, who God is, and what He expects of us.

Jesus said in John 8:31-32, "If you hold to my teachings, you are truly my disciples. Then you will know the truth and the truth will set you free!" David Faust, a Christian minister, educator and writer, gave the following commentary on this verse:

> In what sense does God's truth set us free? It sets us free from the guilt of sin to condemn us to hell. It sets us free from the power of sin to control our lives. It sets us free from the fear of death.
>
> As if all that were not enough, God's truth sets us free from the consequences of a sinful lifestyle. For example, if you hold to the truth of Jesus' Lordship then you will be free from trying to live up to everybody else's expectations. If you

live by what Jesus taught about forgiveness and reconciliation, then you will be free from bitterness and resentment toward others. If you take seriously what Jesus taught about meekness and being poor in spirit, you will be free from self-righteousness and pride. If you heed what Jesus taught us about prayer, you will be free from trying to serve God in your own strength instead of God's strength. If you just look at how Jesus treated people from Samaria, Syro-Phoenicia, or a centurion, you will be free from racism and prejudice. And if you will heed what Jesus taught about moral purity, you will be free from sexual diseases and addictions that weaken bodies, poison minds, and ruin families.

We need to spend time in God's Word every day. Practice what it says. It will set you free!